T0316472

SOME EXERCISES IN
THE
SOUNDS OF SPEECH

Some Exercises in the
SOUNDS OF SPEECH

by

C. C. BELL

Department of Education,
King's College, London

Then said they unto him, Say now Shibboleth: and he said Sibboleth: for he could not frame to pronounce it right. Then they took him, and slew him at the passages of Jordan: and there fell at that time of the Ephraimites forty and two thousand.

Judges xii, 6

CAMBRIDGE

AT THE UNIVERSITY PRESS

1933

CAMBRIDGE
UNIVERSITY PRESS

University Printing House, Cambridge CB2 8BS, United Kingdom

Cambridge University Press is part of the University of Cambridge.

It furthers the University's mission by disseminating knowledge in the pursuit of education, learning and research at the highest international levels of excellence.

www.cambridge.org
Information on this title: www.cambridge.org/9781107585690

© Cambridge University Press 1933

First published 1933
First paperback edition 2015

A catalogue record for this publication is available from the British Library

ISBN 978-1-107-58569-0 Paperback

CONTENTS

PREFACE

This book was conceived as a collection of exercises for practice in spoken English, suitable for the use of students in the Education Department at King's College, London. There is, as far as can be ascertained, no book which provides exercises of the kind required by students training to be teachers, whose aim should be a type of speech acceptable among educated people, and fit for the ears of those who are being educated.

The nonsense rhymes and jingles which undoubtedly have their place in primary and preparatory schools, and the noble numbers provided for students of verse speaking, are alike unsuitable for practice by teachers, whose style of speech in the class-room should vary little from that of ordinary conversation. It is to be regretted that so many of the exercises are in verse form, but it is hard to find examples in prose that provide enough repetition of particular sounds.

Without some knowledge of phonetics, exercises in speech training tend to be purely imitative; the general principles of the study of phonetics and the main problems of speech training have therefore been outlined.

While the book is primarily intended for the use of training college students and teachers, it should be equally useful in secondary schools where speech training in the senior forms aims not merely at "elocution" but at good English in conversation.

The thanks of the author are due to Professor Daniel Jones, of University College, London, who kindly read the typescript and offered valuable suggestions; to Professor J. Dover Wilson, of King's College, London, for his interest and encouragement; and to the following authors and publishers for leave to reproduce passages from copyright poems:

To Macmillan and Co. Ltd. (*Ode on the Death of the Duke of Wellington, The Victim, The Revenge, The Two Voices, Oriana, Oenone, Nothing will die, Charge of the Light Brigade, Charge of the Heavy Brigade, The Merman, In Memoriam*, by Lord Tennyson); to Mr Rudyard Kipling, Messrs A. P. Watt and Son, and Macmillan and Co. Ltd. (*A Charm, A Smuggler's Song, A School Song, Our Fathers of Old, The Heritage*, by R. Kipling); to Lady Gilbert, Mr R. D'Oyly Carte, and Macmillan and Co. Ltd. (*Plays*, by W. S. Gilbert and A. Sullivan); to Dr S. C. Cockerell (*The Earthly Paradise, Sigurd the Volsung*, by W. Morris); to Chatto and Windus (*New Poems, Verses written in* 1872, *Apologetic Postscript*, by R. L. Stevenson).

C. C. BELL

DEVEREUX COURT, W.C. 2
August, 1933

I

INTRODUCTORY

This book is meant for the use of students in training colleges and training departments. While it is greatly to be hoped that in some years' time the effect of speech training in schools will be so widely felt that there will be little necessity for continued instruction after boys and girls leave school, there is at present such a need for this work in training colleges and departments as cannot be supplied in the brief time that is spared for it. Although it may be urged that these students have passed the age at which the best results of training in good speech can be expected, it is clear that every effort must be made to ensure a high standard of speech among teachers, if the results of training in the schools are not to be made nugatory by force of bad example.

By means of the opportunities of what has been called the "educational ladder", a large section of the population of this country to-day has been trained in the use of the King's English, as it is taught in the secondary schools and newer universities. These institutions have often failed to realize an important fact, i.e. that the English spoken in the homes from which their pupils are drawn is not the English in which the writers of English literature themselves thought and spoke. While these schools and colleges have succeeded in teaching written English of a high standard in the matter of vocabulary,

grammar, structure and style, little attention has been
paid to spoken English, with the result that there is
often a wide discrepancy in the effectiveness of tongue
and pen. It is easy to see how this difficulty has been
overlooked, since it is one almost without precedent.
Up till a few years ago, education, except of the most
rudimentary kind, was in general confined to the children
of educated people, whose home circumstances ensured
that ease and fluency in cultured speech which it was
therefore no part of the schools to provide.

The scope of this book is purposely limited; it aims
at providing the essential basis of the theory and practice of good speech, from the point of view only of
phonetic accuracy. Language or speech is much more
than merely a mode of pronunciation. Even in a strictly
limited sense, speech training should include voice production and the aesthetics of speech. In a fuller sense,
it should explore speech as an aspect of personality, and
show the incongruity of any mode of speech which is
not one with the speaker. While no attempt is made
to deal completely or thoroughly with the matter of
breathing or voice production, a few suggestions have
been made in Chapter II with a view to emphasizing
the importance of a technique in breathing "for speech".
Reference is made in the bibliography to works which
deal adequately with this subject.

This book then is concerned with only a small though
essential part of speech training, i.e. pronunciation of
sounds. An attempt has been made, not to lay down
rules as to how sounds *should* be pronounced, but to

show how certain sounds *are* pronounced by a particular group of speakers, and to indicate a way of learning to alter one's own or another person's pronunciation, should one wish to do so. The claims of the particular type of pronunciation described to be regarded as "standard" are discussed in Chapter III.

It should be clearly understood that no amount of theoretical knowledge will take the place of actual practice of speech sounds with the help of an instructor who is able to suggest to the student, by pronunciation, a comparison of the sounds he intends to, and those he in fact does, make. A student whose ear is susceptible to small variations of sound will often correct his own speech with the minimum of theoretical knowledge of phonetics. The exercises in this book are intended as material for practice, but in no way as a substitute for practical work under a competent tutor. Speech training is one of the subjects which cannot be successfully exploited by the purveyors of correspondence courses.

II

BREATHING FOR SPEECH

In the ordinary course of our daily affairs, we do not give much attention to the process of breathing. Our normal actions and conversation do not require us to modify our ordinary effortless intake and outflow of breath; indeed, it is only when we are called upon to make some special physical effort, or when we are suffering from some temporary physical disability affecting the organs of breathing and speech, that we are even conscious of the act of respiration. An athlete or a swimmer is obliged to learn to adapt his breathing process to the physical effort he makes. In the same way, to speak continuously, as in lecturing or teaching, requires some modification of the usual way of breathing.

The familiar breathing exercises of the drill class are not only useless as practice in breathing for speech, but actually make good speech impossible if they are used in this connection. *In the first place*, deep breathing, i.e. complete inflation and deflation of the lungs, is not a desirable practice in speaking. Beginning to speak with the lungs fully inflated makes for a rigidity of the chest and neck muscles, which shows itself in a tenseness of sound, while failure to renew the breath supply before it completely runs out results in inadequate force of breath in the concluding words of a phrase or sentence, and leads to a noisy, gasping sound in the subsequent inhalation. *Secondly*, inhaling through the nose with the mouth shut is a method quite unadapted to breathing for speech, as speaking or reading becomes jerky and discontinuous if the mouth is closed during an intake of breath. (There is no need to dwell upon the effects in speech of any attempt to exhale with the mouth closed.) *Thirdly*, any kind of rigidity of stance, such as standing at attention, prevents the relaxation of neck, chest and shoulder muscles necessary for effective voice production.

Breathing exercises for speech will therefore aim to achieve the following requirements: (1) Intake of breath through the nose and mouth together; (2) Relaxation of the muscles of throat, shoulders and chest; (3) Intake of a breath supply rather greater than that needed for the sentence or phrase to be spoken, and a quiet renewal of breath before the supply is exhausted.

EXERCISES IN BREATHING FOR SPEECH

In speaking or reading, we pause at the end of each "sense group" of words. While we may not need to take in a fresh supply of breath at the end of every such group, we shall not break the sense of any group for the purpose of taking breath. A good speaker or reader, therefore, takes in a breath supply adequate to the length of the group of words he intends to utter, and these groups will vary in length. One of the best exercises, therefore, in breathing for speech is to learn to vary the amount of breath taken in, according to the length of the group of words to be spoken. It should be noted that, since most modern punctuation is based upon grammatical construction rather than upon rhetorical effect, the sense groups will not necessarily coincide with the punctuation of a passage.

Read aloud the following[1] passages, taking breath only where the vertical[2] lines mark the sense pauses:

1. It was a little eminence, remote from any great road, covered with trees and plants of an agreeable verdure, | on the top of which was a stately palace, with a grand and beautiful court in the middle; | within were galleries, and fine apartments elegantly fitted up, and adorned with most curious paintings; | around it were fine meadows, and most delightful gardens, with fountains of the purest and best water. | The vaults also were stored with the richest wines, suited rather to the taste of debauchees, than of modest and virtuous ladies. | This palace they found cleared out, and everything set

[1] In most books of exercises for practice in breathing and speech sounds, the passages are chosen from the finest poems and prose works in the language. Students with any pretensions to literary taste generally dislike the association of great poetry and prose with corrective speech exercises. The extracts in this book have therefore been chosen particularly in the hope of avoiding this offence.

[2] It should be clearly understood that no attempt is here made to indicate a *correct* phrasing of the selected passages: in ordinary reading, the phrasing will vary according to the reader's own preference. The vertical marks merely suggest a grouping which will give useful practice in varying the breath supply.

in order for their reception, | with the rooms all graced with the flowers of the season, to their great satisfaction. |

BOCCACCIO, *The Decameron* (translation)

2. The sport was at its height, the sliding was at the quickest, the laughter was at the loudest, when a sharp smart crack was heard. | There was a quick rush towards the bank, a wild scream from the ladies, and a shout from Mr Tupman. | A large mass of ice disappeared; the water bubbled up over it; Mr Pickwick's hat, gloves and handkerchief were floating on the surface; | and this was all of Mr Pickwick that anybody could see. | Dismay and anguish were depicted on every countenance; the males turned pale, and the females fainted; | Mr Snodgrass and Mr Winkle grasped each other by the hand, and gazed at the spot where their leader had gone down, with frenzied eagerness; | while Mr Tupman, by way of rendering the promptest assistance, and at the same time conveying to any persons who might be within hearing, the clearest possible notion of the catastrophe, | ran off across the country at his utmost speed, screaming "Fire" with all his might. |

DICKENS, *Pickwick Papers*

3. Hence it is almost a definition of a gentleman to say that he is one who never inflicts pain. | This description is both refined and, as far as it goes, accurate. | He is mainly occupied in removing the obstacles which hinder the free and unembarrassed action of those about him; | and he concurs with their movements rather than takes the initiative himself. | His benefits may be

considered as parallel to what are called comforts or conveniences in arrangements of a personal nature; | like an easy chair or a good fire, which do their part in dispelling cold and fatigue, though nature provides both means of rest and animal heat without them. | The true gentleman in like manner carefully avoids whatever may cause a jar or a jolt in the minds of those with whom he is cast; | all clashing of opinion or collision of feeling, all restraint or suspicion, or gloom, or resentment; | his great concern being to make everyone at their ease and at home. | He has his eyes on all his company; he is tender towards the bashful, gentle towards the distant, merciful towards the absurd; | he can recollect to whom he is speaking; he guards against unseasonable allusions, or topics which may irritate; | he is seldom prominent in conversation, and never wearisome. | He makes light of favours while he does them, and seems to be receiving when he is conferring. |

NEWMAN, *The Idea of a University*

4. They gave him a very bad bed-room, and Giglio, when he awoke in the morning, fancying himself in the Royal Palace at home, called, | "John, Charles, Thomas, my chocolate—my dressing-gown—my slippers". But nobody came. | There was no bell, so he went and bawled out for the waiter on the top of the stairs. |

The landlady came up, as cross as two sticks. "What are you shouting for here, young man?" says she. |

"There's no warm water—no servants, my boots are not even cleaned." |

"He, he! Clean 'em yourself", says the landlady. "You young students give yourselves pretty airs. I never heard such impudence." |

"I'll leave the house this instant", says Giglio. |

"The sooner the better, young man. Pay your bill and be off." |

"You may well keep the Bear Inn", said Giglio. "You should have yourself painted as the sign." |

The landlady of the Bear went away growling. |

THACKERAY, *The Rose and the Ring*

5. We have illustrated our meaning by an instance taken from history. We will select another from fiction. | Othello murders his wife; he gives orders for the murder of his lieutenant; he ends by murdering himself. | Yet he never loses the esteem and affection of Northern readers. His intrepid and ardent spirit redeems everything. | The unsuspecting confidence with which he listens to his adviser, the agony with which he shrinks from the thought of shame, | the tempest of passion with which he commits his crimes, and the haughty fearlessness with which he avows them, | give an extraordinary interest to his character. | Iago, on the contrary, is the object of universal loathing. | Many are inclined to believe that Shakespeare has been seduced into an exaggeration unusual with him, and has drawn a monster which has no archetype in human nature. | Now we suspect that an Italian audience in the fifteenth century would have felt very differently. | Othello would have inspired nothing but detestation and con-

tempt. | The folly with which he trusts the friendly
professions of a man whose promotion he had ob-
structed, | the credulity with which he takes unsup-
ported assertions, and trivial circumstances, for un-
answerable proofs, | the violence with which he silences
the exculpation till the exculpation can only aggravate
his misery, | would have excited the abhorrence and
disgust of the spectators. | The conduct of Iago they
would have assuredly condemned; but they would have
condemned it as we condemn that of his victim. |
Something of interest and respect would have mingled
with their disapprobation. | The readiness of the traitor's
wit, the clearness of his judgment, the skill with which
he penetrates the dispositions of others and conceals
his own, would have ensured to him a certain portion
of their esteem. |

MACAULAY, Essay on Machiavelli

6.   The little hedgerow birds,
    That peck along the roads, regard him not. |
    He travels on, and in his face, his step,
    His gait, is one expression: | every limb,
    His look and bending figure, all bespeak
    A man who does not move with pain, but moves
    With thought. | He is insensibly subdued
    To settled quiet; he is one by whom
    All effort seems forgotten; one to whom
    Long patience hath such mild composure given,
    That patience now doth seem a thing of which
    He hath no need. | He is by nature led,

To peace so perfect that the young behold,
With envy, what the Old Man hardly feels. |

WORDSWORTH, *Animal Tranquillity and Decay*

7. Amid these sounds the goodman heard at last
   A song in his own tongue, | and sat upright
   And blinking at the broad bright sun that cast
   A straight beam through the window, making
       bright
   The dusky hangings: | till his gathering sight
   Showed him outside two damsels, pail on head,
   Who went by, singing, to the milking-shed. |

   And meeting them with jingling bit and brace
   Came the grey team from field; | a merry lad
   Sat sideways on the foremost, broad of face,
   Freckled and flaxen-haired, whose red lips had
   A primrose 'twixt them, | yet still blithe and glad,
   With muffled whistle, swinging, did he mock
   The maidens' song and the brown throstle-cock. |

MORRIS, *The Earthly Paradise*

8. We talked of Mr Burke. | —Dr Johnson said,
he had great variety of knowledge, store of imagery,
copiousness of language. | —Robertson. "He has wit
too."—Johnson. "No, sir; he never succeeds there.
'Tis low; 'tis conceit. I used to say, Burke never once
made a good joke. | What I most envy Burke for, is
his being constantly the same. He is never what we
call humdrum; never unwilling to begin to talk, nor

in haste to leave off." | —Boswell. "Yet he can listen."
—Johnson. "No; I cannot say he is good at that. | So
desirous is he to talk, that, if one is speaking at this
end of the table, he'll speak to somebody at the other
end. | Burke, sir, is such a man, that if you met him
for the first time in the street where you were stopped
by a drove of oxen, and you and he stepped aside to
shelter but for five minutes, | he'd talk to you in such a
manner that, when you parted, you would say, this is an
extraordinary man. | Now, you may be long enough
with me, without finding anything extraordinary." |
He said, he believed Burke was intended for the
law; but either had not money enough to follow it,
or had not diligence enough. | He said, he could not
understand how a man could apply to one thing, and
not another. | Robertson said, one man had more judg-
ment, another more imagination. | —Johnson. "No,
sir; it is only, one man has more mind than another.
He may direct it differently; he may, by accident, see
the success of one kind of study, and take a desire to
excel in it. | I am persuaded that, had Sir Isaac Newton
applied to poetry, he would have made a very fine epic
poem. I could as easily apply to law as to tragic
poetry." | —Boswell. "Yet, sir, you did apply to tragic
poetry, not to law." | —Johnson. "Because, sir, I had
not money to study law." |

BOSWELL, *Journal of a Tour to the Hebrides*

9. "They order", said I, "this matter better in
France." | "You have been in France?" said my gentle-

man, turning quick upon me with the most civil
triumph in the world. | "Strange!" quoth I, debating
the matter with myself, "that one and twenty miles
sailing, | for 'tis absolutely no further from Dover to
Calais, | should give a man these rights. I'll look into
them", | so giving up the argument I went straight
to my lodgings, put up half a dozen shirts and a black
pair of silk breeches— | "the coat I have on", said I,
looking at the sleeve, "will do"—took a place in the
Dover stage; | and the packet sailing at nine the next
morning, by three I had got sat down to my dinner
upon a fricaseed chicken, | so incontestibly in France,
that had I died that night of an indigestion, my shirts,
and black pair of silk breeches, portmanteau and all
must have gone to the King of France, | even the little
picture which I have so long worn, and so often have
told thee, Eliza, I would carry with me into my grave, |
would have been torn from my neck. |

STERNE, *A Sentimental Journey*

10. I could not forbear shaking my head and smiling
a little at his ignorance. | And being no stranger to the
art of war, I gave him a description of cannons, culverins,
muskets, carabines, pistols, bullets, powder, swords,
bayonets, battles, sieges, retreats, attacks, undermines,
countermines, bombardments, sea fights; | ships sunk
with a thousand men, twenty thousand killed on each
side; | dying groans, limbs flying in the air, smoke,
noise, confusion, trampling to death under horses' feet;
flight, pursuit, victory; | fields strewed with carcases

left for food to dogs, and wolves, and birds of prey;
plundering, stripping, ravishing, burning, and destroy-
ing. | And to set forth the valour of my own dear
countrymen, I assured him that I had seen them blow
up a hundred enemies at once in a siege, and as many
in a ship, | and beheld the dead bodies come down in
pieces from the clouds, to the great diversion of the
spectators. |

SWIFT, *Gulliver's Travels*

SOME FAULTS OF VOICE PRODUCTION

(a) *Inaudibility*

A common form of inaudibility is that in which the
voice is faint and indistinct at the end of a sentence or
sense group of words. The often heard exhortation
"not to drop the voice" at the close of the sentence is
most misleading. To raise the pitch of the voice will
not make speech any more audible, but will distort the
normal tone and rhythm by altering its natural intonation. A falling intonation is characteristic of many types
of sentence in English, and to tamper with the normal
rise and fall of the voice achieves an effect of arti-
ficiality, often without improving audibility. The reason
behind this kind of inaudibility is usually an inadequate
breath supply for the length of the group of words to
be spoken. Breathing should be subservient to speech;
we should not be obliged to pause for breath where the
sense demands that no pause shall be made. The exercises on pages 6–14 should be practised to remedy this

defect, while the student can easily devise similar exercises for himself.

A different, though hardly less common, form of inaudibility is that in which a speaker simply cannot make himself heard; this kind of inaudibility refers to his speech generally (not as above to an inability to produce a falling intonation clearly), and may be caused in various ways.

(1) Lack of vigour and distinctness in pronunciation of consonants.

(2) Poor flexibility of lip and jaw movement, leading to lack of discrimination between spread and rounded, and open and close vowel sounds.

(3) Lack of vigour in the outflow of breath, resulting in a failure to achieve what speech experts generally refer to as "forward tone".

A good deal of practice is needed in (1) and (2), but little result will be achieved until the defect indicated in (3) is remedied. This kind of "throaty" speech is usually ascribed to defective resonation on the hard palate and teeth ridge, and students of elocution are instructed to "place" the breath forward in the mouth. While it is very doubtful whether this "placing" of the breath in speech can actually occur, there is no doubt that the attempt so to "place" it usually results in greatly increased audibility.

Read or speak a passage aloud, *in a whisper*. As more breath force is needed for whisper than for ordinary speech, this will encourage a vigorous outflow of breath. While whispering, hold one hand extended a few inches away from the mouth. As long as the voice is produced in a "throaty" fashion, there will be little or no sensation of the breath blowing on the hand; as soon as the necessary "forward" production is arrived at, the puffing of the breath will be appreciable. After some practice, a speaker should be able to make himself heard in a whisper across a good-sized room, without feeling any strain.

(b) *Nasality and Lack of Nasal Tone*

In normal English speech, the soft palate is raised so that the breath passes out through the mouth only, except in the formation of the nasal sounds, m, n and ŋ, when the soft palate is lowered and the breath passes out through the nose (the passage through the mouth being obstructed at the lips, teeth ridge or soft palate respectively).

While normally this action of the soft palate takes place without conscious control, some people cannot speak without a certain degree of nasality. This is due to a lack of flexibility of the soft palate, which is never raised enough entirely to cut off some outflow of breath through the nose. This defect is characteristic of cleft palate speech, and is sometimes found as a result of some severe affection of the throat, but when it occurs without apparent physical cause it can generally be remedied by exercises[1] in control of flexibility, i.e. those on page 37, which illustrate nasal plosion.

[1] Reference should be made to Ward, *Defects of Speech*, pub. Dent; Chapter IV on Nasal Twang.

Nasality should not be confused with an inability to produce nasal tone, which is due usually to some congestion of the nasal passages, such as adenoids, and is familiar to most people who have suffered from a severe cold. Lack of nasal tone is generally due to some physical defect, but it can often be remedied by the practice of the same exercises as are recommended above for the correction of undesirable nasality.

III

STANDARD ENGLISH

The type of pronunciation upon which the recommendations and exercises in the following chapters are based is known as Standard English. It is also frequently referred to as Pure English, the King's English (though this term refers more usually to vocabulary and grammatical structure), Good English, Public School English and Received Pronunciation. Although most people have some idea of what is meant by any of these names, the claim of "Standard" to precedence over other forms of English speech demands consideration.

Standard English originated in one of a number of dialects which were spoken in England in past times, and which owed their differences and individual characteristics to the fact that facilities of travel and communication were so slight as to isolate one part of the country from another.

Towards the end of the fourteenth century, the dialect of the East Midland part of the country, with considerable accretions from Southern and other dialects, came to be regarded as the language of learning and culture. The reason is not far to seek. This part of the country included London, Oxford and Cambridge, and was therefore associated with the court, the church, the law, scholarship, letters and the stage. It was also in touch with foreign linguistic influences, which have since had but little effect upon the remoter English dialects. The invention of printing helped to spread this dialect in written form and give it permanence. It is the descendant of this form of English which we now call Standard, and in view of its history we can hardly be surprised to find that it has developed as it were a certain "self-consciousness" as to what is admissible in Standard speech and what is to be rejected.

That Standard speech has for long been the perquisite of an educated minority, and that there has been in the past a definite social cleavage between speakers of Standard English and speakers of other dialects, is no reason for condemning it nowadays as a class luxury. Standard English has a vocabulary richer and a grammar more flexible than any other English dialect, yet the most class-conscious of proletarians has not disdained to profit by the greater fluency that he gains by their study. To take advantage of the grammar and vocabulary of Standard English, while refusing to learn its pronunciation, is as effective as to speak fluently in a foreign language with an English accent. The position is no less incongruous than that of Liza Dolittle in Mr Shaw's *Pygmalion*, who conversely clothed the grammar and vocabulary of Lisson Grove in the accents of a Mayfair drawing-room.

Just as in secondary schools all over England teachers aim at teaching their pupils to write English fluently and effectively, and are content to accept as models nothing less than the finest writings in the language, so must an effort be made to base speech also upon the corresponding models. There is too great a cleavage nowadays between the language a man writes and the language he speaks, and the schools are largely to blame for the incongruity. It is an inharmonious education which trains a man to have something intelligent to say, but provides him with an inappropriate instrument for the saying of it.

Many differing views are held nowadays upon the question of the use of Standard English and dialect. Some hold that modern means of transport and communication have already rung the knell of dialect in this country; that dialects will soon die a natural death; and that it is the part of the schools to anticipate the fact by teaching Standard English and urging its exclusive use. Advocates of this policy have probably not realized the conflict that is almost certain to arise out of such teaching, between home and school. On the other hand, there are many who, realizing the rapid spread of Standard English, would do all in their power to preserve the dialects, feeling that with their disappearance the language would lose something not only of historic interest but of intrinsic charm.

Whatever views we may hold, it is above all important to remember that every man speaks not one language but many languages. We all vary our speech in many ways according to the situation in which we find ourselves; the best speaker is he who is at home in any company. Culture and education are no longer the perquisite of the few; they are very real forces in the life of the nation as a whole. Nowadays, any one who lacks the facility of cultured speech enters the arena with one hand tied to his side. Of no class of persons is this fact more true than it is of teachers.

IV

THE USE OF A PHONETIC TRANSCRIPT

The true use of a phonetic transcript is often misunderstood, and its introduction here must be preceded by a twofold warning. In the first place, the student is in no better position to judge his own speech sounds and correct them after he has learnt the phonetic script than he was before. To learn a symbol ʌ as the vowel sound used in the word "but" will not help him to know whether he pronounces the word "correctly"; nor will it teach him to make any alteration in his way of pronouncing it. Secondly, there is a tendency to attach altogether undue importance to the mere symbols, so that beginners are apt to think they have achieved a knowledge of phonetics when they have in fact done no more than memorize the script.

Although it has already been pointed out with some emphasis, it may be well to assert again that speech training without a competent teacher is a waste of time. The student must learn from the teacher the accredited sound represented by each phonetic symbol. After this, the use of the script becomes clear. Since, in English spelling, one letter or group of letters may represent a variety of sounds (e.g. bough, bought, cough, dough, rough, through), and a single sound may be represented by a variety of spellings (e.g. she, peace, bleed, receive, grieve), it is impossible without phonetic symbols to indicate the pronunciation of sounds, unless constant reference is made to "key" words. It is therefore far simpler and quicker, for the purposes of reference, to have a knowledge of phonetic symbols, merely as "labels", to indicate particular sounds. The pronunciation of the sounds must be learned accurately with the help of a teacher.

The phonetic transcript given below and used hereafter in this book is the "narrow" script of the Association Phonétique Internationale.

The Sounds of English Speech transcribed in Phonetic Symbols

Phonetic symbol	Ordinary spelling of "key" word	Phonetic transcription of "key" word
	Consonants	
p	pan	pæn
b	back	bæk
t	tin	tɪn
d	day	deɪ
k	can	kæn
g	goat	gout
m	mean	min
n	not	nɒt
ŋ	sing	sɪŋ
l	leave	liv
ɫ	tool	tuɫ
f	free	fɹi
v	vote	vout
θ	thin	θɪn
ð	then	ðɛn
s	see	si
z	zest	zɛst
ʃ	show	ʃou
ʒ	pleasure	plɛʒə
ɹ	run	ɹʌn

Phonetic symbol	Ordinary spelling of "key" word	Phonetic transcription of "key" word
h	hand	hænd
w[1]	we	wi
ʍ[1]	when	ʍɛn
j[1]	you	ju
	Vowels and Diphthongs	
i	seat	sit
ɪ	big	bɪg
ɛ	red	ɹɛd
æ	had	hæd
ɑ	palm	pɑm
ɒ	cock	kɒk
ɔ	ford	fɔd
ʊ	good	gʊd
u	boot	but
ʌ	but	bʌt
ɜ	bird	bɜd
ə	about	əbaʊt
eɪ	wake	weɪk
oʊ	cold	koʊld
aɪ	fight	faɪt
aʊ	round	ɹaʊnd
ɔɪ	boy	bɔɪ
ɪə	near	nɪə
ɛə	chair	tʃɛə
ɔə	bore	bɔə
ʊə	poor	pʊə

[1] These sounds are often known as semi-vowels, partaking as they do of the nature of both vowels and consonants.

V

TESTING AND COMPARING SOUNDS

The sounds of English speech may be conveniently divided into two main groups of consonants and vowels. The English vowel sounds are formed by the outward passage of voice[1] through the mouth, without such obstruction or narrowing as to cause audible friction. In the formation of consonants, the sound may be either voiced or voiceless, and there is always such obstruction or narrowing as to cause audible friction.

Below will be found in tabular form lists of words containing the various English consonant sounds, following and preceding the various English vowel sounds. These lists will be found useful for testing students' pronunciation of Standard English. They may also be used, together with the various exercises suggested, for practice of the sounds illustrated.

---

[1] The difference between breath and voice is due to the action of the vocal cords. These cords in the larynx are drawn close together in the formation of certain speech sounds, when they vibrate and cause what is known as "voice". All vowel sounds are voiced, and certain consonant sounds, such as b, d, g, v, ð, z and ʒ. These consonants have their voiceless, or breathed, equivalents, p, t, k, f, θ, s and ʃ, corresponding exactly in formation, except for the position of the vocal cords.

VOWEL SOUNDS PRECEDED BY CONSONANT SOUNDS

	i	ɪ	ε	æ	ɑ	ɒ	ɔ	ʊ	u	ʌ	ɜ
(Initially)	eat	inn	end	at	aunt	off	all	—	—	under	urge
p	peak	pip	pest	pad	past	pond	pall	put	pool	pun	pearl
b	beat	bit	bend	band	bar	box	board	bull	boot	butter	burn
t	tease	tick	ten	tank	task	top	talk	took	tool	tusk	turn
d	dean	dish	desk	dapper	dark	dock	daughter	—	do	Dutch	dirty
k	keen	kick	kept	catch	card	copper	caulk	could	coot	cup	curse
g	geese	gimlet	guest	gap	gasp	god	gaudy	good	goose	gun	girl
m	meat	miss	mess	mat	mark	mock	Maud	mullah[3]	moose	mother	murky
n	neat	nip	neck	nag	nasty	notch	north	nook	noon	nut	nurture
ŋ	—	—	—	—	—	—	—	—	—	—	—
l	leak	list	leather	latch	last	lot	lord	look	loot	lunch	learn
f	feast	fist	fender	fat	far	fop	fork	full	fool	fuss	fur
v	veal	village	very	van	vast	vault[2]	vaunt	—	voodoo	vulture	virtue
θ	thief	thick	Thespian	thank	—	thong	thought	—	—	thunder	third
ð	these	this	then	that	—	—	—	—	—	thus	—
s	seam	sister	send	sand	sark	soft	sought	soot	soon	supper	serve
z	zeal	zinc	zest	Zanzibar	—	—	—	—	Zoo	—	—
ʃ	sheet	ship	shell	shack	shark	shot	shawl	should	shoot	shut	sherbet
[d +ʃ]³ ʒ¹	congeal	gist	jelly	jam	jar	jot	Jordan	Judaea	June	judge	jerk
r	reach	rip	rent	rag	hurrah	rotten	raucous	rook	rude	rust	—
h	heat	hip	head	happen	harsh	hock	hoard	hood	hoop	hunt	hurt
w	wean	win	wet	wax	—	want	ward	wood	woo	wonder	work
ʍ	wheat	which	when	whack	—	what	wharf	—	—	—	whirl
j	yeast	Yiddish	yellow	yak	yard	yacht	yawl	yucca	you	young	yearn

¹ The sound ŋ is not found initially in English.　² Or volt.　³ Or mala.

VOWEL SOUNDS PRECEDED BY CONSONANT SOUNDS (continued)

	ə	eɪ	oʊ	aɪ	aʊ	ɔɪ	ɪə	ɛə	ɔə	ʊə
(Initially)	arrive	aid	oak	eye	oust	oyster	ear	air	oar	—
p	perhaps	pain	poke	pipe	pout	point	pier	pair	pour	poor
b	believe	bake	bone	bite	bound	boy	beer	bear	bore	boor
t	to-night	taste	tone	time	tout	toil	tier	tear	tore	tour
d	derive	date	dole	dyke	doubt	doyley	dear	dare	door	doer
k	correct	cake	coke	kite	cow	coil	kier	care	core	—
g	gavotte	gape	goat	guide	gown	goitre	gear	garish	gore	gourd
m	meringue	make	mope	might	mound	moist	mere	mare	more	moor
n	necessity	nape	note	night	now	noise	near	ne'er	Nore	—
ŋ	—	—	—	—	—	—	—	—	—	—
l	lobelia²	late	lobe	like	lout	loin	leer	lair	lore	lure
f	ferment	fate	phone	fine	found	foil	fear	fair	four	—
v	verbena	vain	vote	viper	vouch	voice	veer	vair	—	—
θ	author	thane	—	thigh	thousand	—	theatre	—	thaw	—
ð	leather	they	those	thine	thou	—	—	there	—	—
s	suppose	sake	soak	sight	sound	soil	sear	—	sore	sure
z	zenana	zany	zodiac	Zion	—	—	vizier	—	—	jury
ʃ	rasher	shake	show	shine	shout	—	sheer	share	shore	—
[d+ʒ] ʒ¹	jerboa	jade	joke	gibe	joust	joint	jeer	—	jaw	—
r	receive³	rake	rope	ripe	rout	roister	rear	rare	roar	—
h	heredity	haste	hope	height	how	hoist	hear	hair	hoar	houri
w	—	wait	woe	wipe	wound	—	weird	wear	war	—
ʍ	—	whale	—	white	—	—	—	where	—	—
j	lawyer	Yale	yoke	—	—	yoicks	year⁴	yare	yore	sewer

¹ The sound ʒ is not found initially in English. ² Or lobitlja. ³ Or ɹɪsiv. ⁴ Or jɜ.
⁵ Some speakers would pronounce the vowels in all the words below as ɔ. Many would pronounce some as ɔ, and others as ɔə.

VOWEL SOUNDS FOLLOWED BY CONSONANT SOUNDS

	i	ɪ	ɛ	æ	ɑ	ɒ	ɔ	u	ʊ	ʌ	ɜ
(Finally)	he	—	—	—	bar	—	core⁷	do	—	—	her
p	heap	ship	rep	tap	carp	shop	pauper	soup	—	cup	purple
b	glebe	nib	neb	cab	barb	hob	daub	tube	—	snub	herb
t	seat	hit	met	rat	cart	cot	sought	coot	foot	hut	hurt
d	read	bid	said	bad	lard	rod	board	food	good	mud	bird
k	meek	wick	wreck	hack	park	lock	hawk	spook	look	luck	lurk
g	league	rig	peg	bag	saga	bog	auger	fugue	sugar	mug	burg
m	team	dim	hem	lamb	calm	bomb	storm	boom	room	come	sperm
n	scene	tin	pen	man	barn	shone	corn	moon	—	fun	burn
ŋ	—	sing	—	pang	—	long	—	—	—	flung	—
l	feel	will	tell	pal	marl	doll	wall	cool	pull	gull	curl
f	leaf	skiff	clef	gaff	laugh	scoff	dwarf	roof	—	rough	turf
v	leave	sieve	—	spavin	halve	of	dwarves	move	—	dove	serve
θ	heath	myth	death	hath	bath	broth⁵	forth	truth	—	doth	birth
ð	breathe	with	whether	lather	father	bother	—	soothe	—	brother	further
s	niece	hiss	less	mass	pass	oss⁶	force	loose	puss	fuss	curse
z	sneeze	his	says	jazz	vase	because	cause	lose	hussar	buzz	hers
ʃ	leash	wish	mesh	rash	harsh	bosh	—	barouche	bush	hush	nasturtium
ʒ	seizure¹	—	pleasure	azure²	garage³	—	—	rouge	—	—	—
r	—	Syria	merry	carry	tarry⁴	sorrow	story	—	hurrah	hurry	furry
h	—	—	—	—	—	—	—	—	—	—	—
w	—	—	—	—	—	—	—	—	—	—	—
ʍ	—	—	—	—	—	—	—	—	—	—	—
j	—	—	—	—	—	—	—	—	—	—	—

¹ Or siːzjuə, or siːʒuə.　² Or æʒjuə, or eʒjuə, or ezʒjuə.　³ Or the more recent, Anglicized gæːrɪdʒ.　⁴ Adjective, from tar.　⁵ Or brɔθ.　⁶ Or ɔs.　⁷ Or kɔə.

VOWEL SOUNDS FOLLOWED BY CONSONANT SOUNDS (continued)

	ə	eɪ	oʊ	aɪ	aʊ	ɔɪ	ɪə	ɛə	ɔə	ʊə
(Finally)	mariner	pay	go	eye	bow	boy	beer	hair	four[4]	poor
p	hiccup	cape	hope	type	—	—	—	—	—	—
b	Arab	babe	globe	tribe	—	—	—	—	—	—
t	carrot	bait	coat	fight	bout	quoit	fiat	—	—	—
d	mustard	raid	load	side	loud	buoyed	beard	laird	—	—
k	haddock	lake	joke	like	gowk	—	—	—	—	—
g	—	plague	vogue	rigor	—	—	—	—	—	—
m	bottom	lame	home	lime	—	—	—	—	—	—
n	flatten	bane	cone	shine	town	coin	lien	cairn	—	—
ŋ	—	—	—	—	—	—	—	—	—	—
l	moral	hale	whole	mile	fowl	boil	—	—	—	cruel
f	seraph	safe	loaf	wife	—	—	—	—	—	—
v	caravan	rave	rove	drive	—	—	—	—	—	—
θ	Marathon	rathe	both	python	mouth	—	—	—	—	—
ð	—	bathe	loathe	tithe	mouth[3]	—	—	—	—	—
s	palace[1]	race	dose	dice	house	joist	—	—	—	—
z	hammers	haze	doze	size	rouse	boys	tiers	bears	fours[5]	tours
ʃ	—	satiated[2]	kosher	—	—	—	—	—	—	—
ʒ	—	azure	—	—	—	—	—	—	—	—
h	correct	Ahab	cohort	—	—	—	—	—	—	tourist
w	rehearse	—	—	—	—	—	—	—	—	—
ʍ	away	—	—	—	—	—	—	—	—	—
j	—	—	—	—	—	—	—	—	—	—

[1] Or pælis. [2] See note 2 on p. 27. [3] Verb. [4] Or fɔ. [5] Or fɔz.

VI

THE ENGLISH CONSONANTS

Consonants are classified according to (a) the nature
of the obstruction or narrowing which takes place in
their formation, and (b) that part of the articulatory
tract[1] at which such obstruction or narrowing occurs.
Thus, the consonants may be

(1) *plosive*, in which the breath is momentarily stopped
and then released,

(2) *nasal*, in which the breath passes through the nose
instead of through the mouth,

(3) *lateral*, in which the breath passes round an obstruction which partly blocks its passage,

(4) *fricative*, in which the breath passage is not actually
stopped but so narrowed as to cause audible
friction.

These obstructions or narrowings may occur at
various points in the articulatory tract. English consonant sounds are therefore referred to as

(1) *bi-labial*, in which the obstruction is formed by the
lips,

(2) *labio-dental*, in which the narrowing occurs between
the upper teeth and lower lip,

[1] In ordinary English speech, this extends from the lips to
the velum (soft palate), but see page 38 for the use of the
glottal stop and page 88 for uvular sounds.

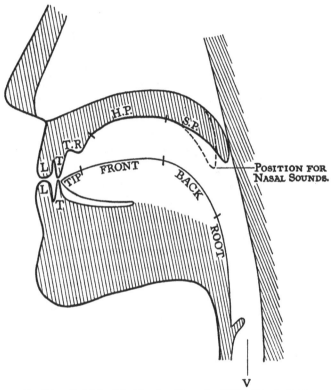

L. Lip, Labial; T. Teeth, Dental; T.R. Teeth Ridge,
Alveolar; H.P. Hard Palate, Palatal; S.P. Soft Palate or Velum,
Velar; V. Vocal Cords, Glottal.

(3) *dental*, in which the narrowing occurs between the tip of the tongue and the upper teeth,

(4) *alveolar*, in which the obstruction or narrowing occurs between the tip or blade of the tongue and the upper teeth ridge,

(5) *palato-alveolar*, in which the obstruction or narrowing occurs between the tip or blade of the tongue and the teeth ridge, while the front of the tongue is raised towards the hard palate,

(6) *velar*, in which the obstruction occurs between the back of the tongue and velum (soft palate),

(7) *glottal*, in which the narrowing takes place between the vocal cords.

The following table shows the English consonant sounds arranged according to the classification explained above:

	Bi-labial	Labio-dental	Dental	Alveolar	Palato-alveolar	Velar	Glottal
Plosive	p b	—	—	t d	—	k g	—
Nasal	m	—	—	n	—	ŋ	—
Lateral	—	—	—	l ɫ	—	—	—
Fricative	—	f v	θ ð	s z ɹ	ʃ ʒ	—	h

In suggesting exercises for practice in consonant articulation, it is well to distinguish between faulty and defective articulation. As this book is meant for students training to be teachers, it should be unnecessary to consider the grosser forms of speech defects, such as cleft palate speech, lisping, etc. Reference is made in the list of books on page 87 to an excellent book on this subject. The exercises in this book will therefore be confined to those which attempt to remedy careless or over-precise pronunciation. (But see the appendix on this subject.)

VII

EXERCISES IN CONSONANT PRACTICE

(a) *Plosive Consonants*

The pronunciation of t and d will sometimes need correction in the speech of careless speakers. These sounds, when pronounced without much vigour, tend to be followed by a rubbing (fricative) sound, so that t sounds like ts, and d like dz. This can best be remedied by practising very vigorous articulation, removing the tongue quickly from the teeth ridge as soon as contact has been made. Practice will also be needed to avoid a similar slovenly articulation of tr and dr. Less commonly, the other plosive consonants, p, b, k and g, need correction in the same way.

Exercises for Practice of Plosive Consonants

i	tea	meat	treacle	dean	bead	dream
ɪ	tin	sit	trip	dip	hid	drip
ɛ	tell	bet	trench	desk	bed	dread
æ	tack	cat	trap	dapper	sad	drab
ɑ	tar	heart	—	dark	lard	draught
ɒ	top	lot	tropic	dock	god	drop
ɔ	tall	sport	trawler	daughter	lord	draw
ʊ	took	foot	—	—	good	—
u	tool	boot	truth	do	food	drool
ʌ	ton	cut	trust	dust	mud	drunk
ɜ	turn	hurt	—	dirt	curd	—
ə	lantern	parrot	trepan	depart	wandered	dragoon
eɪ	take	fate	tray	date	paid	dray
oʊ	toast	coat	trophy	dope	load	drove
aɪ	tight	height	trite	dine	hide	dry
aʊ	town	lout	trout	down	proud	drought

Exercises for Practice of Plosive Consonants (continued)

ɔɪ	toil	quoit	Troy	Doyle	decoyed	—
ɪə	tier	theatre	—	deer	feared	drear
ɛə	tear	—	—	dare	cared	—
ɔə	tore	—	—	door	—	drawer
ʊə	tour	—	truer	doer	endured	—

Two return tickets to Tooting.
He took a trip by tram to Tring.
I shall try to travel on the two-twenty.
"Double, double, toil and trouble."
Dreadful and distressing dreams.
"Dare to be a Daniel."
Daily deliveries at the door.
Deeds of derring-do.

A cup of Cadbury's cocoa.
Going to Gravesend in a gig.
A couple of carbon copies required.
Clerk to the County Council.
Post the parcel promptly.
Proposals that appear practicable.
"Builds bonny babies."
Bunyan's *Pilgrim's Progress*.
Backed for a place.

> I cannot tell how the truth may be;
> I say the tale as 'twas said to me.
>
> SCOTT, *The Lady of the Lake*

If you want a receipt for that popular mystery
Known to the world as a Heavy Dragoon,

Take all the remarkable people in history,
Rattle them off to a popular tune....
Take of these elements all that is fusible,
Melt 'em all down in a pipkin or crucible,
Set 'em to simmer and take off the scum,
And a Heavy Dragoon is the residuum.

GILBERT, Patience

And broader still became the blaze, and louder still
    the din,
As fast from every village round the horse came spur-
    ring in:
And eastward straight from wild Blackheath, the war-
    like errand went,
And raised in many an ancient hall the gallant squires
    of Kent.   MACAULAY, The Armada

I know the kings of England and I quote the fights
    historical,
From Waterloo to Marathon, in order categorical;
I'm very well acquainted too with matters mathematical,
I understand equations, both the simple and quadratical.

GILBERT, The Pirates of Penzance

(b) Unexploded Plosive Consonants

The consonants p, b, t, d, k and g are known as
plosives, because in pronouncing them we momentarily
stop the breath and then release it with plosion. In
certain circumstances, however, these consonants are
to be regarded as stops,[1] but not as plosives; i.e. the

---

[1] This is literally true only of a plosive which is followed
by a consonant articulated in exactly the same position as the

breath is stopped, but another consonant sound follows immediately instead of the plosion.

1. When one plosive consonant immediately follows another, the first of the two loses its plosion and becomes a stop; e.g. map-book, hat-trick, egg-cup, lap-dog, nutcracker. (This should not be confused with words *spelt* with a double consonant but pronounced with a single sound; e.g. happy.)

2. Similarly, when a plosive consonant is immediately followed by a nasal consonant, it is customary to pronounce the plosive as a stop followed by nasal plosion; e.g. shopman, oatmeal. This pronunciation includes words in which a plosive is followed by its equivalent nasal consonant, separated in spelling by an unstressed vowel only; i.e. p or b + m [1], t or d + n, k or g + ŋ [1]; e.g.

> mutton will be pronounced mʌtn, not mʌtən,
> sudden   ,,   ,,   sʌdn, not sʌdən.

first; e.g. map-book, hat-trick, shopman. When the second consonant is articulated in a different position from the first, there is unavoidably a very slight plosion of the first consonant almost simultaneously with that of the second. For all practical purposes, however, the first of the two consonants may be regarded as a stop.

[1] It will be noted that instances of these combinations do not ordinarily occur in educated speech. There are instances, however, in which by assimilation the influence of the preceding plosive has changed the following nasal, so that it corresponds in position to the preceding plosive, which is then pronounced as a stop, followed by nasal plosion, e.g. open > oʊpm, instead of oʊpn; bacon > beɪkŋ, instead of beɪkn. This is on the whole not a pronunciation to be recommended.

Elocutionists often recommend the plosion of the first consonant in these instances, but it is regarded as stilted and affected by most educated speakers, who would no more think of saying gʊdʰ dɒg, than they would of saying faɪvʰ fiŋgəz, or ðɪsʰ sɒŋ. Speakers who use this somewhat artificial pronunciation of plosives should examine their speech to find out whether they are guilty of a similar articulation of other than plosive consonants.

Exercises for Practice of Unexploded Plosive Consonants

map-book	stopped	nutcracker	doctor
cup-bearer	swept	hat brim	cooked
top boy	rat-trap	hat-box	expect
stop-press	act two	white cat	waked
apt	bad dog	hot-bed	wagged
inept	hat-trick	hat-pin	picked
escaped	sit down	egg-cup	milk-bottle
lap-dog	lost dog	book-case	sackbut
robbed	pet dog	actor	stockpot
sobbed	kit-bag		

Exercises for Practice of Nasal Plosion

beaten	madden	straighten	Edna
Eton	sadden	laden	Rodney
wheaten	harden	maiden	Courtney
bitten	begotten	oaken	chutney
kitten	cotton	oaten	Putney
written	rotten	rodent	Stepney
bidden	sodden	heighten	liftman
hidden	broaden	widen	oatmeal
ridden	warden	cabman	litmus
Armageddon	Luton	shopman	utmost
deaden	button	topmast	madman
redden	mutton	helpmeet	batman
batten	Sutton	kidney	Hackney
fatten	certain	Sydney	weakness
patten	curtain	Etna	bagman
gladden	burden		

(c) The Glottal Stop and other Intrusive Sounds

The glottal stop (ʔ) is a sound used by many speakers of English, but as it is intrusive and in no way an essential sound in English speech it has not been included in the table of consonant sounds. It is a plosive consonant, formed in the glottis by the stoppage and subsequent release of breath between the vocal cords. Many speakers use the glottal stop in certain circumstances without being themselves aware of the fact, but it is for the most part not countenanced by educated usage. The commonest instances of its use are as follows:

1. Before a word beginning with a vowel, generally where the word bears special emphasis, e.g. How awful! (hau ʔɔfəl). Though not usually regarded as a vulgarism, this use of the glottal stop is generally considered aesthetically undesirable.

2. Instead of a plosive consonant, between vowels or before another consonant, e.g. letter, pronounced lɛʔə, instead of lɛtə; bottle, pronounced bɒʔl, instead of bɒtl.

3. To bridge the gap between two vowel sounds, e.g. India Office, pronounced ɪndjəʔ ɒfɪs, instead of ɪndjə ɒfɪs.

Exercises for Practice in Avoiding the Glottal Stop

1. Practise these exercises at first with the sound of h preceding each word. Later, without actually pronouncing h, say the word after the outflow of breath has begun.

i	eagerly	Easter	evening
ɪ	ill	illustrated	ink
ɛ	anywhere	end	ever
æ	accurate	anxiously	average
ɑ	arbour	ark	ask
ɒ	honest	office	olive
ɔ	awful	order	ordinary
ʊ	—	—	—
u	Oudh	ousel	—
ʌ	onion	under	utterly
ɜ	earl	earnest	urge
ə	about	agreeable	around
eɪ	ache	aged	ale
oʊ	ogle	open	over
aɪ	ice	idle	island
aʊ	owl	oust	out
ɔɪ	oil	ointment	oyster
ɪə	ear	eerie	Erin
ɛə	air	airy	aerial
ɔə	oar	—	—
ʊə	—	—	—

2. Practise these exercises by pronouncing the words with a pause before the consonant for which the glottal stop is substituted. Gradually shorten the pause until the word is normally pronounced.

i	Peter	beetle	seeker	—	sleepy[1]	steeple
ɪ	fitting	kitten	flicker	fickle	skipping	tipple
ɛ	letter	petrol	wrecking	reckless	stepping	Stepney
æ	Saturn	mattress	sacking	Hackney	happy	chapman
ɑ	carter	startle	marking	sparkle	harpist	—
ɒ	whatever	bottle	stocking	Cockney	poppy	shopman
ɔ	porter	fortress	talker	—	—	—
ʊ	footer	—	looking	—	—	—
u	scooter	footling	—	—	stooping	—
ʌ	mutter	chutney	lucky	Lucknow	puppy	—
ɜ	dirty	myrtle	lurking	—	chirping	—
ə	return	retrieve	—	lacrosse	suppose	—
eɪ	waited	waitress	baker	sacred	draper	—

[1] The glottal stop is hardly ever substituted for p in this position, but is pronounced simultaneously with p.

ou	photograph	total	focus	vocal	soapy	—
aɪ	writing	title	liking	Michael	piper	—
au	scouting	—	—	—	—	—
ɔɪ	loiter	—	—	—	—	—
ɪə	theatre	—	—	—	—	—
ɛə	—	—	—	—	—	—
ɔə	—	—	—	—	—	—
uə	—	—	—	—	—	—

3. In attempting to eradicate the glottal stop, be careful to avoid other intrusive sounds, such as (*a*) intrusive r,[1] e.g. ɪndjəɹ ɒfɪs; (*b*) intrusive j, e.g. aɪj æm. This is a semi-vowel, similar in formation to the vowel i, but made in a closer position so as to cause slight friction. To avoid this intrusion, pronounce the first of the two adjacent vowels with less vigour; (*c*) intrusive w, e.g. tuw ɛgz. This is also a semi-vowel, similar to the vowel u in formation, but made in a closer position. Adopt a method similar to that suggested for avoidance of intrusive j.

Avoid intrusive r	Avoid intrusive j	Avoid intrusive w
china egg	we ask	you are
India Office	she always does	two eggs
the idea of it	three acts	few ever do
manna and quails	they are	new ornaments
cinema artist	I am	blue overcoats
law of libel	by omnibus	too ornate
a flaw in it	tie up	true honesty
gondola oar	spy out	how interesting
Joanna Arden	joy eternal	so eager
he saw it	toy umbrella	go out
Lama of Tibet	boy ushers	no object
	pay out	
	may I	
	high odds	

[1] Some authorities on speech consider that the intrusive r is now so firmly entrenched in English speech that it is not only pedantic but useless to attempt to dislodge it.

(d) Sounds corresponding to the Letter l

It should be noted that there are two sounds corresponding to the letter l in English speech. These are the "clear" l, used before vowels, and the "dark" ɫ,[1] used finally and before consonants. Clear l is pronounced with the tip of the tongue against the teeth ridge, as shown in figure 1. Dark ɫ is pronounced with the tip of the tongue in the same position as for clear l, but with the back of the tongue raised to the position of a vowel sound, as shown in figure 2.

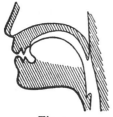
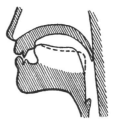

Fig. 1.   Fig. 2.

Compare the pronunciation of the clear and dark l's in the word "little" (lɪtɫ).

The raising of the back of the tongue varies individually from the position of ɔ to that of ʊ, though a fairly close[2] position is characteristic of educated speech.

[1] In many people's speech the sound ɫ has a distorting effect upon a stressed vowel immediately preceding, especially upon i and ou (which in Cockney speech, for instance, are often heard as ɪ and ɒʊ respectively). This fact should be borne in mind when practising vowel sounds followed by ɫ.

[2] For meaning of "close" and "open" vowel sounds, see page 45.

In pronouncing dark ɫ, careless speakers often raise the back of the tongue to a half-open position, and omit contact of the tongue tip with the teeth ridge. In an attempt to counteract this tendency, many elocutionists insist on a clear l in all positions. Such a pronunciation sounds stilted and over-precise, and should be avoided equally with the careless pronunciation noted above.

In certain dialects, notably in the English of Wales, the clear l is used in all positions. A dark ɫ may be learnt by trying to pronounce the vowel sound ʊ simultaneously with clear l. The words bull, full, pull, wool, may then be practised, holding the tongue position of ʊ while the following ɫ is pronounced.

Exercises for Practice of Clear and Dark l

	l initially	l between vowels	ɫ finally	ɫ followed by a final consonant
i	lead	mealy	feel	field
ɪ	list	silly	bill	milk
ɛ	leper	telephone	tell	help
æ	lad	shallow	pal	talc
ɑ	last	barley	marl	gnarled
ɒ	long	solid	loll	revolve
ɔ	lawn	bawling	ball	bald
ʊ	look	pullet	full	pulled
u	loom	cooler	tool	ruled
ʌ	luck	mullet	dull	bulk
ɜ	learn	early	pearl	hurled
ə	legitimate	quarrelling	oral	herald
eɪ	ladle	sailor	mail	hailed
oʊ	load	holy	coal	fold
aɪ	like	dilute	file	mild
aʊ	loud	howling	fowl	howled
ɔɪ	loiter	boiler	toil	soiled
ɪə	leer	realistic	real	—
ɛə	lair	fairly	—	—
ɔə	law	—	—	—
ʊə	—	surely	cruel	fuelled

Other Examples of Dark ɫ

p	help	please	purple
b	bulb	bless	bubble
t	colt	—	hurtle
d	sealed	—	muddle
k	bulk	clean	sparkle
g	amalgamate	glow	gargle
m	helm	—	mammal
n	Colne	—	funnel
l	wholly	—	—
ɫ	self	fly	shuffle
v	solve	—	shovel
θ	health	—	lethal
s	else	slow	hustle
z	bells	—	teasle
ʃ	Welsh	—	—

Let the bell be toll'd;
And a deeper knell[1] in the heart be knoll'd;
And the sound of the sorrowing anthem roll'd
Thro' the dome of the golden cross;
And the volleying cannon thunder his loss;
He knew their voices of old.

TENNYSON, *Ode on the Death of the Duke of Wellington*

Therefore they shall do my will
To-day while[1] I am master still,
And flesh and soul, now both are strong,
Shall hale the sullen slaves along.

HOUSMAN, *A Shropshire Lad*

The hollow winds begin to blow,
The clouds look black, the glass is low,
The soot falls down, the spaniels sleep.

JENNER, *Signs of Rain*

[1] Either ɫ finally, or l followed by a vowel without any considerable pause.

Let him the lion first control,
And still the tiger's famish'd growl.
Let us, like them, our freedom claim,
And make him tremble at our name.

GAY, *The Council of Horses*

With an old study fill'd full of learned old books,
With an old reverend chaplain, you might know him by
his looks.

ANON., *The Old Courtier*

A perilous life, and sad as it may be,
Hath the lone fisher, on the lonely sea,
O'er the wild water labouring far from home,
For some bleak pittance e'er compelled to roam.

CORNWALL, *The Fisherman*

Ellen, I am no courtly lord,
But one who lives by lance and sword,
Whose castle is his helm and shield,
His lordship the embattled field.

SCOTT, *The Lady of the Lake*

VIII

THE ENGLISH VOWELS

The vowel sounds of English may be classified according to the position of the tongue and the lips in their formation.

1. *Tongue Position.* In the pronunciation of vowel sounds, part of the tongue is raised towards the roof of the mouth. Vowels are therefore classified according to (*a*) the part of the tongue which is raised, and (*b*) the degree of raising which takes place.

(*a*) *Front* vowels are those in the formation of which the front part of the tongue is raised towards the front part of the hard palate, e.g. i, in "bead".

Central vowels are those in the formation of which the middle part of the tongue is raised towards the back part of the hard palate, e.g. ɜ, in "stern".

Back vowels are those in the formation of which the back part of the tongue is raised towards the soft palate, e.g. u, in "pool".

(*b*) When the tongue is raised into a position so close to the palate as almost to cause friction, the sound is said to be a "close" vowel, e.g. i and u.

When the tongue is raised very little, so as to leave some considerable space between the palate and the tongue, the sound is called an "open" vowel.

The intermediate positions are known as "half-close" and "half-open".

English Vowel Sounds

	Front	Central	Back
Close	i ɪ	—	u ʊ
Half-close	e* ɛ	з	o†
Half-open	—	—	ɔ ʌ
Open	æ a‡	a§	ɑ ɒ

* e the starting point of the diphthong eɪ.

† o   ,,   ,,   ,,   oʊ.

‡ a   ,,   ,,   ,,   aɪ.

§ a   ,,   ,,   ,,   aʊ. The same first symbol is used in transcribing aɪ, aʊ, although their starting points differ slightly.

2. *Lip Position.* The position of the lips varies from spread to fully rounded, according to the vowel sound which is being pronounced. The lips are most fully spread for i (as in "bead") and most fully rounded for u (as in "pool"). Although a large number of inter-mediate positions between the extremes are used, it is customary to classify lip position for the pronunciation of vowels as (1) spread, (2) neutral, (3) openly rounded, (4) closely rounded.

The English vowel sounds fall under the following headings: Spread, i, ɪ; Less widely spread, ɛ; Spread to Neutral, æ; Neutral, з, ə, ʌ; Neutral to Openly rounded, ɑ; Openly rounded, ɒ; Rounded, ɔ; Closely rounded, ʊ, u.

It will be noted that close tongue position is ac-companied by full spreading or rounding of the lips, and open tongue position by an approximation to the neutral lip position. The spreading of the lips is characteristic of front vowels; the rounded position, of back vowels; and the neutral position, of central vowels.

No attempt to describe the formation of the vowel sounds of Standard English will be altogether satisfactory, owing to the very considerable variation in pronunciation to be found among educated speakers. A speaker might easily be found, for instance, whose speech sounds did not in any one instance *exactly* correspond to the sounds described below. There is, however, to be observed a certain relation and proportion between one sound and another in the pronunciation of good speakers, so that the following descriptions, although they may not accurately represent the exact pronunciation of every speaker of good English, are nevertheless valuable in indicating the appropriate interval between one sound and another. Thus a speaker whose pronunciation of u is rather closer than that suggested in the description below will probably find that his o, ɔ and ɒ have a corresponding tendency to closeness of formation. It is extremely important to realize this fact in attempting to "correct" a dialectal pronunciation of English, since the alteration of isolated sounds, without regard to their position in the student's pronunciation as a whole, will generally result in artificial and ill-balanced speech.

The following descriptions, then, are intended to represent a form of Standard English based not so much upon any one model of speech as upon the relative position of one sound to another.

1. i　Close, front vowel, with spread lip position.
2. ɪ　Between close and half-close, somewhat centralized front vowel, with spread lip position.
(The pronunciation of this vowel varies to some extent according to its position in the word. Many speakers pronounce a more open sound before ɫ and in a final position. Cf. "bit" with "bill", and the two sounds in "busy".)
3. ɛ　About half-way between close and open, front vowel, with slightly spread lip position.
4. æ　Rather less than fully open, front vowel, with neutral to slightly spread lip position.
5. ɑ　Fully open, somewhat centralized back vowel, with neutral lip position.
6. ɒ　Open, back vowel, with slight openly rounded lip position.
7. ɔ　Between open and half-open, back vowel, with considerably rounded lip position.
8. ʊ　Between close and half-close, somewhat centralized back vowel, with closely rounded lip position.
9. u　Close, back vowel, with closely rounded lip position.
10. ʌ　Between open and half-open, somewhat centralized back vowel, with neutral lip position.
11. ɜ　About half-way between close and open, central vowel, with neutral lip position.
12. ə　Half-open, central vowel, with neutral lip position.

(This sound varies a good deal in pronunciation, being the unstressed form of many different vowel sounds. Its position varies, according to the degree of absence of stress, along a line connecting the stressed form with the central neutral sound ə, described above.)

13. eɪ The tongue starts from a somewhat closer position than that of the pure vowel ɛ, and moves towards the position of ɪ.

14. oʊ The tongue starts from a half-close, somewhat centralized back vowel position, and moves towards the position of ʊ.

(There is considerable variation in the pronunciation of this sound, according to the amount of (1) lip-rounding, and (2) centralization, of the first element.)

15. aɪ The tongue starts from a fully open, slightly centralized front vowel position, and moves towards the position of ɪ.

16. aʊ The tongue starts from an open, somewhat centralized back vowel position, and moves towards the position of ʊ.

17. ɔɪ The tongue starts from a slightly more open position than that of the pure vowel ɔ, and moves towards the position of ɪ.

18. ɪə The tongue starts from the position of the pure vowel ɪ, and moves towards the position of ə.

19. ɛə The tongue starts from a somewhat more open position than that of the pure vowel ɛ, and moves towards the position of ə.

20. ɔə The tongue starts from a slightly more open
            position than that of the pure vowel ɔ, and
            moves towards the position of ə.

        (This sound does not occur at all in the speech
            of many educated persons, who use in its
            place the pure vowel ɔ.)

21. ʊə The tongue starts from the position of the pure
            vowel ʊ, and moves towards the position of ə.

It would be impossible, within the scope of this
book, to enumerate and classify the many dialectal
variants of the foregoing Standard English vowel
sounds. Reference should be made to Chapters x and xi
of Ward's *The Phonetics of English*, where the matter is
treated in detail. Below an attempt is made to record
some of the sounds which are found in Cockney speech.

It should be noted that there are many differences in
pronunciation within the limits of Cockney, but that
these may be roughly divided into "broad", i.e. uneducated Cockney, and "refined", i.e. literate, but not
cultured speech. The latter type of speech is usually
found among persons whose aim is to discard or avoid
the "broad" dialect, as unfitted to their social position.

It is interesting to observe that some of these "refined" Cockneyisms apparently represent so eager a
desire to turn away from what is regarded as vulgar that,
phonetically speaking, they have overshot the mark, and
vary as much from Standard English in the one direction as the "broad" Cockney does in the opposite. For
instance, the Standard English diphthong aɪ is pronounced in "broad" Cockney with its first element

retracted, and sometimes slightly raised, i.e. ɑɪ or ɒɪ. Thus, "five" becomes fɑɪv or fɒɪv. The "refined" speaker, in his anxiety to avoid this pronunciation, uses a sound approximating to æɪ (fæɪv), the Standard English sound aɪ representing a point about midway between the two extremes. Similarly, the Standard English diphthong aʊ becomes, in one form of "broad" Cockney, æʊ, whereas in "refined" Cockney the sound is pronounced ɑʊ.

VOWEL SOUNDS HEARD IN "BROAD" COCKNEY SPEECH, WITH SUGGESTIONS AS TO HOW TO CORRECT THEM

Almost all Cockney vowel sounds show some degree of nasality, notably the open ones, and particularly ɑ. As this fault will need separate correction from those of tongue and lip position, no further reference to nasality is made in the corrective suggestions outlined below. But see page 16.

It will often be found that a student can correct his own sounds merely by hearing and imitating the correct ones. Let this be done whenever possible; it is unnecessary to give instructions as to tongue and lip positions to any one able to effect an alteration by ear.

1. i   The sound is diphthongized, approximating to
        əɪ, with less lip spreading than in the Standard
        sound; e.g. me = məɪ.
        The sound should be formed with a great deal
        of vigour, the tongue being raised to the close
        position before any sound is uttered. Lips
        should be spread.

4-2

  Before ɪ, the sound becomes ɪ; e.g. meal = mɪɫ, or with slight diphthongization ɪə.

  It is better to omit practice of the sound before ɪ until it can be pronounced with ease in other contexts.

2. ɪ In a final position, the sound is diphthongized approximately to əɪ; e.g. happy = hæpəɪ.

  See page 83 for corrective suggestions.

3. ɛ The sound is formed in a close position, approximating to e, and often lengthened; e.g. bed = bed.

  If this sound is too close, it will almost certainly be found that æ is also too close. Therefore, let the student aim at pronouncing something like his own æ sound.

  Before ɪ, the sound is often greatly retracted, resulting in a pronunciation something like ɔ; e.g. well = wɔɫ.

  To correct retraction, the student must attempt a forward and rather closer vowel sound, and should pronounce ɪ with the back of the tongue in a rather close position. See page 41.

4. æ The sound is formed in a close position, often almost indistinguishable from Standard ɛ; e.g. cab = kɛb.

  Avoid lip spreading; tend to drop the lower jaw slightly in pronouncing the sound.

5. ɑ The back of the tongue is raised approximately to the ɒ position, while the length of Standard ɑ is retained; e.g. father = fɒðə.

The sound should be corrected by pronouncing it with slightly spread lips, and by relaxing any tension of the tongue, so that it assumes a fully open position.

6. ɒ In some words, ɔ is substituted for ɒ, with considerable lengthening; e.g. cough = kɔf.

The lips should be kept in as nearly the neutral position as possible, and the back of the tongue slightly lowered. The vowel should be pronounced without lengthening.

7. ɔ There is a tendency to pronounce the sound in too close a position; e.g. bought = bot. Where the sound is final, there is a tendency to diphthongize the vowel. Thus Standard ɔ may become oə; e.g. paw = poə.

The mouth should be opened rather wide, to avoid close lip rounding, while to eliminate the diphthong the mouth must not be moved during the pronunciation of the sound.

8. ʊ Before ɫ, there is a tendency to retract the sound, so that it resembles o; e.g. pull = poɫ.

The lips should be fully rounded, and the tongue position should be closer and more nearly central.

9. u This sound becomes centralized, and sometimes diphthongized, so that it approximates to ü or ïü;[1] e.g. moon = mün or mïün.

The front of the tongue must not be raised, but kept down immediately behind the lower

[1] ¨ over a vowel indicates a tendency to centralize the sound.

front teeth. The back of the tongue should be pushed well back, and the sound pronounced with some vigour.

Before ɨ, the sound usually approximates to o; e.g. cool = koɫ.

To remedy this, the lips should be fully rounded and the back of the tongue raised as vigorously as possible to an extremely close position.

10. ʌ   The sound becomes fronted, and is pronounced rather like a, often with considerable lengthening; e.g. cut = kat.

It should be pronounced short, without any tendency to lip spreading, and an attempt made to retract the tongue in the direction of ɒ.

Before ɨ, the tongue is raised and retracted, so that it approximates to a sound between ɔ and o; e.g. bulky = boɫkɪ.

To correct this pronunciation, avoid all lip rounding, and lower the tongue in the direction of a.

11, 12. ɜ, ə   These sounds show little variation from the Standard form.

13. eɪ   The first element of the diphthong becomes centralized and often very considerably more open than in Standard; e.g. lake = ləɪk or laɪk.

The sound is best corrected by attempting to raise the tongue further in the direction of the second element of the diphthong before pronouncing the first element.

Before ɨ, the second element becomes centralized, so that the sound approximates to aə e.g. dale = daəɨ.

It is better to omit practice of words ending in ɨ until the eɪ sound can be made in other contexts. ɨ should then be pronounced with a close position of the back of the tongue. See page 41.

14. oʊ There are various Cockney forms of this sound, the chief being those approximating to ʌʊ, æʊ and ëʊ̈; e.g. hope = hʌʊp, hæʊp or hëʊ̈p.

To correct ʌʊ, aim at a closer first element, as near as possible to ɜ with lip rounding; when the necessary close position has been achieved, attempt to retract the sound to o.

To correct æʊ or ëʊ̈, aim at a pure o sound and, only when this has been achieved, attempt to add the second element of the diphthong with additional lip rounding.

15, 16. aɪ, aʊ For descriptions, see pages 50 and 51.

These sounds may be corrected by substituting the first element of aʊ for that of aɪ, and vice versa. In point of fact, the sound will be near enough to Standard if one intermediate sound is used as the first element in both these diphthongs.

There is another Cockney pronunciation of aʊ, in which the sound is monophthongized as a, with considerable lengthening; e.g. round = ɹand.

This is best corrected by pronouncing the sound without undue lengthening, and adding ʊ, with considerable lip rounding.

17. ɔɪ Not much variation is found.

18, 19. ɪə, ɛə The first elements of the diphthongs become i and e respectively, often separated from the second elements by j; e.g. fear = fi(j)ə, and there = ðe(j)ə.

To correct this, the first element must be pronounced with a lower tongue position and with less vigour, so that there is a gentle glide towards the second element. See page 40 on "intrusive j and w".

20, 21. ɔə, ʊə The first elements of the diphthongs become o and u respectively, and are often separated from the second elements by w; e.g. four = fo(w)ə, and tour = tu(w)ə.

For corrective suggestions, see 18 and 19 above.

IX

EXERCISES IN VOWEL PRACTICE

1. i

The land is sick, the people diseased,
And blight and famine on all the lea:
The holy Gods, they must be appeased,
So I pray you tell the truth to me.

TENNYSON, *The Victim*

I can see the shadowy lines of its trees,
    And catch in the sudden gleams,
The sheen of the far-surrounding seas,
And islands that were the Hesperides
    Of all my boyish dreams.

LONGFELLOW, *My Lost Youth*

And party leaders you might meet
In twos and threes in every street
Maintaining with no little heat
    Their various opinions.

GILBERT, *The Gondoliers*

Fair with golden sheaves,
Rich with the darkened autumn leaves,
Gay with the water-meadows green,
The bright blue stream that lay between,
The mile of beauty stretched away
From that bleak hill-side bare and gray.

MORRIS, *The Man Born to be King*

These shall show thee treasure hid,
Thy familiar fields amid;
And reveal (which is thy need)
Every man a king indeed.

KIPLING, *A Charm*

Don't let them know she liked them best,
　For this must ever be
A secret kept from all the rest,
　Between yourself and me.

CARROLL, *Alice in Wonderland*

Through the green twilight of a hedge
I peered with cheek on the cool leaves pressed,
And spied a bird upon a nest:
Two eyes she had beseeching me
Meekly and brave.

DE LA MARE, *The Mother Bird*

2. 1

In the green and gallant Spring,
Love and the lyre I thought to sing
And kisses sweet to give and take
By the flowery hawthorn brake.

STEVENSON, *New Poems*, No. LXV

His mind is concrete and fastidious,
　His nose is remarkably big;
His visage is more or less hideous,
　His beard it resembles a wig.

LEAR, *Nonsense Songs and Stories*

Come, fill the cup, and in the Fire of Spring
The Winter Garment of Repentance fling:
The Bird of Time has but a little way
To fly—and Lo! the Bird is on the Wing.
FITZGERALD, Rubaiyat of Omar Khayyam

I can set a braggart quailing with a quip,
The upstart I can wither with a whim;
He may wear a merry laugh upon his lip,
But his laughter has an echo that is grim.
When they're offered to the world in merry guise,
Unpleasant truths are swallowed with a will—
For he who'd make his fellow-creatures wise
Should always gild the philosophic pill.
GILBERT, The Yeomen of the Guard

Hop and skip to Fancy's fiddle,
Hands across and down the middle,
Life's perhaps the only riddle
    That we shrink from giving up.
GILBERT, The Gondoliers

Folk say, a wizard to a northern king
At Christmas-tide such wondrous things did show,
That through one window men beheld the spring....
MORRIS, The Earthly Paradise

3. ɛ

A more humane Mikado never
    Did in Japan exist,
To nobody second, I'm certainly reckoned
    A true philanthropist.

It is my very humane endeavour
    To make, to some extent,
Each evil liver a running river
    Of harmless merriment....
And make each prisoner pent
Unwillingly represent
    A source of innocent merriment,
    Of innocent merriment.

GILBERT, The Mikado

The eldest Oyster looked at him,
    But never a word he said:
The eldest Oyster winked his eye,
    And shook his heavy head—
Meaning to say he did not choose
    To leave the oyster-bed.

CARROLL, Alice through the Looking-Glass

For he said "Fight on! Fight on!"
Tho' his vessel was all but a wreck;
And it chanced that when half of the short summer
    night was gone,
With a grisly wound to be drest he had left the deck,
But a bullet struck him that was dressing it suddenly dead,
And himself he was wounded again in the side and the
    head.

TENNYSON, The Revenge

Now sleeping once on a day of marvellous fire,
A brood of snakes he had cherished in grave regret
That death his people had dealt their dam and their sire,
Through savage dread of them, crept to his neck and set
Their tongues to lick him.

MEREDITH, Melampus

He is not dead, this friend—not dead,
But, in the path we mortals tread,
Got some few, trifling steps ahead,
    And nearer to the end,
So that you, too, once past the bend,
Shall meet again, as face to face, this friend
    You fancy dead.

STEVENSON, *Verses Written in* 1872

The boy stood on the burning deck
    Whence all but he had fled.
The flame that lit the battle's wreck
    Shone round him o'er the dead.

HEMANS, *Casabianca*

4. æ

He listen'd and look'd; it was only the cat;
But the Bishop he grew more fearful for that,
For she sat screaming, mad with fear,
At the army of rats that was drawing near.

SOUTHEY, *Bishop Hatto*

Smack went the whip, round went the wheels,
    Were never folk so glad;
The stones did rattle underneath
    As if Cheapside were mad.

COWPER, *John Gilpin*

Lord Chancellors were cheap as sprats,
And Bishops in their shovel hats
Were plentiful as tabby cats—
    If possible, too many.

GILBERT, *The Gondoliers*

Just as he said this, what should hap
At the chamber door but a gentle tap?
"Bless us," cried the Mayor, "What's that?
Anything like the sound of a rat
Makes my heart go pit-a-pat."
BROWNING, The Pied Piper of Hamelin

Trample! trample! went the roan,
  Trap! trap! went the gray;
But pad! pad! pad! like a thing that was mad,
  My chestnut broke away....
Pad! pad! they came on the level sward,
  Thud! thud! upon the sand;
With a gleam of swords and a burning match,
  And a shaking of flag and hand.
THORNBURY, The Cavalier's Escape

So, with the throttling hands of Death at strife,
  Ground he at grammar;
Still, through the rattle, parts of speech were rife,
  While he could stammer.
BROWNING, A Grammarian's Funeral

5. ɑ

Sir Richard spoke, and he laugh'd, and we roar'd a
  hurrah, and so
The little Revenge ran on sheer into the heart of the foe.
TENNYSON, The Revenge

When I, good friends, was called to the Bar
  I'd an appetite fresh and hearty,
But I was, as many young barristers are,
  An impecunious party.   GILBERT, Trial by Jury

The pibroch sounds, the bands advance,
The broadswords gleam, the banners dance,
Obedient to the Chieftain's glance.

SCOTT, The Lady of the Lake

Five and twenty ponies,
    Trotting through the dark—
Brandy for the Parson,
    'Baccy for the Clerk.
Them that asks no questions isn't told a lie—
Watch the wall, my darling, while the Gentlemen go by!

KIPLING, A Smuggler's Song

The scouts had parted on their search,
    The Castle gates were barr'd;
Above the gloomy portal arch,
Timing his footsteps to a march,
    The Warder kept his guard.

SCOTT, Marmion

6. D

Time, however his wheels we may clog,
Wends steadily still with onward jog,
And the cock-tail'd puppy's a curly-tail'd dog.

BARHAM, The Bagman's Dog

It was twelve by the village clock
When he crossed the bridge into Medford town.
He heard the crowing of the cock
And the barking of the farmer's dog,
And felt the damp of the river fog,
That rises after the sun goes down.

LONGFELLOW, Paul Revere's Ride

And then he'd sing so blithe and jolly;
   Ah, many's the time and oft!
But mirth is turned to melancholy,
   For Tom is gone aloft.

               DIBDIN, *Tom Bowling*

I might forget my weaker lot;
For is not our first year forgot?
The haunts of memory echo not.

               TENNYSON, *The Two Voices*

In varying cadence, soft or strong,
He swept the sounding chords along:
The present scene, the future lot,
His toils, his wants, were all forgot:
Cold diffidence, and age's frost,
In the full tide of song were lost.

               SCOTT, *The Lady of the Lake*

7. ɔ

The Warders with their shoes of felt
   Crept by each padlocked door,
And peeped and saw, with eyes of awe,
   Grey figures on the floor.

               WILDE, *Ballad of Reading Gaol*

They are not to be told by the dozen or score,
But by thousands they come, and by myriads and more;
Such numbers had never been heard of before,
Such a judgment had never been witnessed of yore....

And in at the windows and in at the door,
And through the walls helter-skelter they pour,
And down from the ceiling and up through the floor,
From the right and the left, from behind and before.

SOUTHEY, *Bishop Hatto*

I lighted down my sword to draw,
I hackéd him in pieces sma',
I hackéd him in pieces sma',
   For her sake that died for me.

ANON., *Helen of Kirconnell*

His horse, who never in that sort
   Had handled been before,
What thing upon his back had got
   Did wonder more and more.

COWPER, *John Gilpin*

The morning breaks; the steeds in their stalls
Stamp and neigh, as the hostler calls;
The day returns; but nevermore
Returns the traveller to the shore;
   And the tide rises, and the tide falls.

LONGFELLOW, *The Tide Rises, the Tide Falls*

She stood upon the castle wall,
She watched my crest among them all,
She saw me fight, she heard me call,
When forth there stept a foeman tall,
Between me and the castle wall.

TENNYSON, *Oriana*

8. ʊ

The stubborn spearmen still made good
Their dark impenetrable wood,
Each stepping where his comrade stood
    The instant that he fell.

SCOTT, Marmion

The Cardinal rose with a dignified look,
He call'd for his candle, his bell, and his book.

BARHAM, The Jackdaw of Rheims

His lord's command he ne'er withstood,
Though small his pleasure to do good.
As the corslet off he took,
The dwarf espied a Mighty Book!
Much he marvell'd a knight of pride
Like a book-bosom'd priest should ride.

SCOTT, The Lay of the Last Minstrel

As from some blissful neighbourhood,
A notice faintly understood,
"I see the end, and know the good".

TENNYSON, The Two Voices

9. u

Thus, if a king were coming, would we do;
And 'twere good reason too;
For 'tis a duteous thing
To show all honour to an earthly king.

Christ Church MS.

Who for such dainties would not stoop?
Soup of the evening, beautiful soup!

CARROLL, Alice in Wonderland

The mute expression served in lieu of confession,
And, being thus coupled with full restitution,
The Jackdaw got plenary absolution.

BARHAM, *The Jackdaw of Rheims*

Step and prop-iron, bolt and screw,
Spring, tire, axle, and linchpin too,
Steel of the finest, bright and blue, . . .
That was the way he put her through—
"There," said the Deacon, "now she'll do".

HOLMES, *One-Hoss Shay*

Indeed a rich and savoury stew 'tis;
    And true philosophers, methinks,
Who love all sorts of natural beauties,
    Should love good victuals and good drinks.

THACKERAY, *The Ballad of Bouillabaisse*

O river, while thy waters roll
    By yonder vast deserted tomb,
There, where so clear a soul
    So shone through gathering doom,
    Thou and thy land shall keep the tale of lost Khartoum.

NEWBOLT, *The Nile*

10. A

The knight's bones are dust,
His sword is rust,
His soul is with the saints, I trust.

COLERIDGE, *The Knight's Tomb*

And ere three shrill notes the pipe uttered,
You heard as if an army muttered;
And the muttering grew to a grumbling;
And the grumbling grew to a mighty rumbling;
And out of the houses the rats came tumbling.

BROWNING, *The Pied Piper of Hamelin*

'Tis morn; but scarce yon level sun
Can pierce the war-clouds, rolling dun,
Where furious Frank and fiery Hun
  Shout in their sulphurous canopy.

CAMPBELL, *Hohenlinden*

Our feelings we with difficulty smother,
  When constabulary duty's to be done.
Oh, take one consideration with another!
  A policeman's lot is not a happy one.

GILBERT, *The Pirates of Penzance*

You see, of course, if you're not a dunce,
How it went to pieces all at once,—
All at once, and nothing first,—
Just as bubbles do when they burst.

HOLMES, *One-Hoss Shay*

I have beheld him tremble oft enough
At things he could not choose but trust to me,
Although he knew the world was wise and rough;
And never did he fail to let me see
His love.

MORRIS, *The Earthly Paradise*

Prayer unsaid, and mass unsung,
Deadman's dirge must still be rung.

DARLEY, *Deadman's Dirge*

II. 3

When those words were heard, that poor little bird
Was so changed in a moment, 'twas really absurd.

BARHAM, *The Jackdaw of Rheims*

All the little boys and girls,
With rosy cheeks and flaxen curls,
And sparkling eyes and teeth like pearls.

BROWNING, *The Pied Piper of Hamelin*

Some beneath the further stars
  Bear the greater burden:
Set to serve the land they rule,
(Save he serve no man may rule,)
Serve and love the lands they rule;
  Seeking praise nor guerdon.

KIPLING, *A School Song*

Now he patted his horse's side,...
Then, impetuous, stamped the earth,
And turned and tightened his saddle-girth;
But mostly he watched with eager search
The belfry-tower of the Old North Church.

LONGFELLOW, *Paul Revere's Ride*

To think we buy gowns lined with ermine
For dolts that can't or won't determine
What's best to rid us of our vermin!

BROWNING, *The Pied Piper of Hamelin*

Why should we yet our sail unfurl?
There's not a breath the blue wave to curl.

Moore, Canadian Boat Song

Then to this earthen Bowl did I adjourn
My Lip the secret Well of Life to learn:
And Lip to Lip it murmured—"While you live
Drink! for once dead you never will return".

FitzGerald, Rubaiyat of Omar Khayyam

12.[1] ə

"'Tis strange, my friend; the Kingfisher
But yestermorn conjured me here
Out of his green and gold to say
Why thou, in splendour of the noon,
Wearest of colour but golden shoon,
And else dost thee array
In a most sombre suit of black."

De la Mare, The Riddle

And, strange to say, the sons of pleasure,
They who have revelled beyond measure
In beauty, wassail, wine, and treasure,
Die calm, or calmer, oft than he
Whose heritage was misery.

Byron, Mazeppa

In the greenest of our valleys
    By good angels tenanted,
Once a fair and stately palace—
    Radiant palace—reared its head.

[1] See also exercises for practice of vowels in unstressed
syllables, on page 83.

In the monarch Thought's dominion—
    It stood there!
Never seraph spread a pinion
    Over fabric half so rare.

POE, The Haunted Palace

Still she spake on and still she spake of power,
"Which in all action is the end of all;
Power fitted to the season; wisdom bred
And throned of wisdom—from all neighbour crowns
Alliance and allegiance, till thy hand
Fail from the sceptre-staff".

TENNYSON, Œnone

13. eɪ

And or ever that evening ended a great gale blew,
And a wave like the wave that is raised by an earth-
    quake grew.

TENNYSON, The Revenge

    When I remember'd again
    How my Philip was slain,
    I wept and I wail'd,
    The tears down hail'd,
    But nothing it avail'd
    To call Philip again
    Whom Gib our cat hath slain.

SKELTON, Lament for Philip Sparrow

Which is why I remark,
And my language is plain,
That for ways that are dark,
And for tricks that are vain,
The heathen Chinee is peculiar—
Which the same I am free to maintain.

BRET HARTE, *That Heathen Chinee*

The world was never made;
It will change, but it will not fade,
So let the wind rage.

TENNYSON, *Nothing will Die*

But, in spite of all temptations
To belong to other nations,
   He remains an Englishman.

GILBERT, *H.M.S. Pinafore*

I remember the sea-fight far away,
   How it thundered o'er the tide!
And the dead captains, as they lay
In their graves, o'erlooking the tranquil bay,
   Where they in battle died.

LONGFELLOW, *My Lost Youth*

There is a chamber far away
   Where sleep the good and brave,
But a better place ye have named for me
   Than by my father's grave.

AYTOUN, *The Execution of Montrose*

A man who would woo a fair maid
Should 'prentice himself to the trade,
  And study all day
  The methodical way,
How to flatter, cajole, and persuade.

GILBERT, The Yeomen of the Guard

14. ou

I weep, for it reminds me so
Of that old man I used to know—
Whose look was mild, whose speech was slow,
Whose hair was whiter than the snow,
Whose face was very like a crow,
With eyes, like cinders, all aglow,
Who seemed distracted with his woe,
Who rocked his body to and fro,
And muttered mumblingly and low,
As if his mouth were full of dough,
Who snorted like a buffalo—
That summer evening long ago
  A-sitting on a gate.

CARROLL, Alice through the Looking-Glass

Broke through the mass from below,
Drove through the midst of the foe,
Plunged up and down, to and fro,
Rode, flashing blow upon blow.

TENNYSON, The Charge of the Heavy Brigade

O Lady fair and sweet
Arise and let us go
Where comes not rain or snow,
Excess of cold or heat,
To find a still retreat
By willowy valleys low
Where silent rivers flow.

STEVENSON, *New Poems*, No. LXXVI

Pat as a sum in division it goes—
(Every plant had a star bespoke)—
Who but Venus should govern the Rose?
Who but Jupiter own the Oak?
Simply and gravely the facts are told
In the wonderful books of our fathers of old.

KIPLING, *Our Fathers of Old*

There lived a King, as I've been told,
In the wonder-working days of old,
When hearts were twice as good as gold,
And twenty times as mellow.

GILBERT, *The Gondoliers*

Who would be
A merman bold,
Sitting alone,
Singing alone
Under the sea,
With a crown of gold,
On a throne?

TENNYSON, *The Merman*

The Bellman perceived that their spirits were low,
  And repeated in musical tone
Some jokes he had kept for a season of woe—
  But the crew would do nothing but groan.

CARROLL, The Hunting of the Snark

15. aɪ

As I ride, as I ride
To our Chief and his Allied,
Who dares chide my heart's pride
As I ride, as I ride?
Or are witnesses denied—
Through the desert waste and wide
Do I glide unespied
As I ride, as I ride?

BROWNING, Through the Metidja to Abd-el-Kadi

They feed you till you want to die
On rhubarb pie and pumpkin pie,
And horrible huckleberry pie,
And when you summon strength to cry,
"What is there else that I can try?"
They stare at you in mild surprise
And serve you other kinds of pies.

BELLOC, New Cautionary Tales

I am tired of living singly
On this coast so wild and shingly—
I'm aweary of my life;
If you'll come and be my wife,
Quite serene would be my life.

LEAR, Nonsense Songs

In enterprise of martial kind,
When there was any fighting,
He led his regiment from behind—
He found it less exciting.

GILBERT, The Gondoliers

Whene'er I poke
Sarcastic joke
  Replete with malice spiteful,
The people vile
Politely smile,
  And vote me quite delightful!
Now when a wight
Sits up all night
  Ill-natur'd jokes devising
And all his wiles
Are met with smiles,
  It's hard, there's no disguising!

GILBERT, Princess Ida

But though the compliment implied
Inflates me with legitimate pride,
It nevertheless can't be denied
That it has its inconvenient side.

GILBERT, Iolanthe

16. au

That was the year when Lisbon town
Saw the earth open and gulp her down,
And Braddock's army was done so brown,
Left without a scalp to its crown.

HOLMES, One-Hoss Shay

There's a cry and a shout, and a deuce of a rout,
And nobody seems to know what they're about,
But the monks have their pockets all turned inside out.

BARHAM, The Jackdaw of Rheims

Old as the Rhine of great renown,
    She hurries clear and fast,
She runs amain by field and town,
From south to north, from up to down,
    To present on from past.

STEVENSON, New Poems, No. CII

King James, the while, with princely powers,
Holds revelry in Stirling towers.
Soon will this dark and gathering cloud
Speak on our glens in thunder loud.
Inured to bide such bitter bout,
The warrior's plaid may bear it out.

SCOTT, The Lady of the Lake

Were not this well, to bide mine hour,
Tho' watching from a ruin'd tower
How grows the day of human power?

TENNYSON, The Two Voices

But he was very stiff and proud:
He said, "You needn't shout so loud".

CARROLL, Alice through the Looking-Glass

So sinketh the din and the tumult; and the earls of the
    Goths ring round
That crown of the kings of battle laid low upon the
    ground.

MORRIS, The Story of Sigurd the Volsung

Where weeping birch and willow round
With the long fibres swept the ground,
Here, for retreat in dangerous hour,
Some chief had framed a rustic bower.

SCOTT, *The Lady of the Lake*

17. ɔː

Speak roughly to your little boy,
    And beat him when he sneezes:
He only does it to annoy,
    Because he knows it teases.

CARROLL, *Alice in Wonderland*

And wherefore rather I made choice
To commune with that barren voice,
Than him that said, "Rejoice! Rejoice!"

TENNYSON, *The Two Voices*

The pot began to bubble and boil;
The old man cast in essence and oil,
He stirred all up with a triple coil
    Of gold and silver and iron wire,
Dredged in a pinch of virgin soil,
    And fed the fire.

C. ROSSETTI, *The Prince's Progress*

The harp, his sole remaining joy,
Was carried by an orphan boy.

SCOTT, *The Lay of the Last Minstrel*

18. ɪə

For all behind was dark and drear,
And all before was night and fear.

BYRON, *Mazeppa*

But, owing, I'm much disposed to fear,
    To his terrible taste for tippling,
That highly respectable Gondolier
Could never declare with a mind sincere
Which of the two was his offspring dear,
    And which the Royal stripling.

GILBERT, *The Gondoliers*

When the lawn is shaven clear,
Then my hole shall reappear,
I shall find him, never fear.
I shall find my grenadier.

STEVENSON, *The Dumb Soldier*

Woe to the wretch who fails to rear
At this dread sign the ready spear!
For, as the flames this symbol sear,
His home, the refuge of his fear,
    A kindred fate shall know.

SCOTT, *The Lady of the Lake*

If you see this song, my dear,
    And last year's toast,
I'm confoundedly in fear
You'll be serious and severe
    About the boast.

STEVENSON, *Apologetic Postscript*

To arms they flew,—axe, club, or spear,—
And mimic ensigns high they rear,
And, like a banner'd host afar,
Bear down on England's wearied war.

SCOTT, *The Battle of Bannockburn*

Meanwhile, his friend, through alley and street,
Wanders and watches with eager ears,
Till in the silence around him he hears...
...the measured tread of the grenadiers.

LONGFELLOW, *Paul Revere's Ride*

19. ɛə

All shrank, like boys who unaware,
Ranging the woods to start a hare,
Come to the mouth of the dark lair
Where, growling low, a fierce old bear
    Lies amid bones and blood.

MACAULAY, *Horatius*

Flash'd all their sabres bare,
Flash'd as they turn'd in air
Sabring the gunners there.

TENNYSON, *The Charge of the Light Brigade*

The Upper School had combed and oiled their hair,
And all the Parents of the Boys were there.

BELLOC, *A Moral Alphabet*

Hearts just as pure and fair
May beat in Belgrave Square
As in the lowly air
Of Seven Dials.

GILBERT, *Iolanthe*

For many a busy hand toil'd there,
Strong pales to shape, and beams to square,
The lists' dread barriers to prepare.

SCOTT, *The Lay of the Last Minstrel*

Before them stood a guilty pair;
But, though an equal fate they share,
Yet one alone deserves our care.

SCOTT, *Marmion*

20. ɔə

For examples of exercises in the practice of this sound, see page 64. See also pages 26 and 50.

21. ʊə

Wherefore through them is freedom sure;
    Wherefore through them we stand
From all but sloth and pride secure,
    In a delightsome land.

KIPLING, *The Heritage*

And just as I became assured
My lame foot would be speedily cured,
The Music stopped.

BROWNING, *The Pied Piper of Hamelin*

"The thing can be done," said the Butcher, "I think.
    The thing must be done, I am sure.
The thing can be done! Bring me paper and ink,
    The best there is time to procure."

CARROLL, *The Hunting of the Snark*

A nice little boy held a golden ewer,
Emboss'd and fill'd with water as pure
As any that flows between Rheims and Namur.
                    BARHAM, *The Jackdaw of Rheims*

O living will that shalt endure
    When all that seems shall suffer shock,
    Rise in the spiritual rock,
Flow through our deeds and make them pure.
                    TENNYSON, *In Memoriam*

VOWELS IN UNSTRESSED SYLLABLES

In unstressed syllables, vowels tend to lose their distinctive quality, and become "obscure" or neutral sounds. In certain dialects, however, vowels in unstressed syllables retain their distinctive quality; thus, many Northern speakers will pronounce the word "success" as sʌksɛs, whereas most Southern speakers would use the form səksɛs. It is sometimes erroneously believed that these Northern speakers stress the unstressed syllable, but this is not the case. Compare the Northern speaker's pronunciation of ˈɒbdʒɛkt (noun), and ɒbˈdʒɛkt (verb); the two are easily distinguished by their characteristic stresses. It is easy to see how this misconception arises, when we realize that Southern speakers associate distinctive vowel quality with position in a stressed syllable and will therefore be apt to assume a stressed syllable wherever a vowel of distinctive quality is heard.

The most common substitute for any vowel in an unstressed syllable is the neutral sound ə, but many educated speakers use ə in some instances and ɪ in others.

The relative strength or weakness of the vowel sound used in an unstressed syllable depends a good deal upon the circumstances. In recitation or formal speech, the sound will approximate to the strong form from which the weak is derived, rather than to the "obscure" neutral form of rapid and colloquial speech. See page 49.

Exercises for Practice of Vowels in Unstressed Syllables

Pronounced ə		Pronounced ə or ɪ	
absorb	occur	captain	legitimate
assume	perhaps	carpet	modesty
attention	petition	charity	mountain
caress	picture	chicken	nearest
common	regulation	decree	object (noun)
confess	romance	depart	palace
doctor	sailor	effect	policy
golden	soldier	escape	receive
human	success	fountain	regret
maiden	themselves	happiness	repeat
object (verb)	to-morrow	heareth	rushes
obscure	until	houses	
obtain	useful		

For additional exercises for practice of vowels in unstressed syllables, see page 70.

ɪ IN FINAL POSITION

The sound ɪ (usually spelt y) when it occurs finally is often pronounced əɪ by careless speakers, a form of pronunciation usually associated with uneducated speech. This tendency is probably due to lack of vigour in formation; instead of pronouncing a pure sound (a somewhat close front vowel with spread lip position; see page 48 for detailed description), the speaker diphthongizes the sound, starting from a central position and moving in the direction of ɪ. The formation of the sound is thus begun in a more central and more open position than is required.

Many elocutionists try to counteract this tendency by recommending the use of the more fronted sound ɛ, but this usage has a stilted and artificial effect. However, a speaker who starts the ɪ sound from too central a position may be urged to "think towards" ɛ in attempting to correct his error.

Exercises for Practice of ɪ in a Final Position

Examples of ɪ finally

	after a stressed syllable	after an unstressed syllable
p	happy	canopy
b	baby	Araby
t	pretty	charity
d	lady	parody
k	whisky	finicky
g	shaggy	—
m	dreamy	enemy
n	many	balcony
ŋ	springy	—
l	ably	merrily
f	leafy	atrophy
v	heavy	—
θ	healthy	—
ð	smithy	—
s	mercy	fallacy
z	hazy	fantasy
ʃ	bushy	—
ʒ	stodgy	Lalage
ɹ	very	chicory
h	—	—
w	—	—
ʍ	—	—
j	—	—

Then, if you plan it, he
Changes organity,
With an urbanity
Full of Satanity,
Vexes humanity
With an inanity
Fatal to vanity,
Driving your foes to the verge of insanity.

GILBERT, *The Sorcerer*

He gave us all a goodbye cheerily
    At the first dawn of day;
We dropped him down the side full drearily
    When the light died away.

NEWBOLT, *Messmates*

Touch her not scornfully;
Think of her mournfully,
    Gently and humanly....
Ere her limbs frigidly
Stiffen too rigidly,
Decently, kindly,
    Smooth and compose them.

HOOD, *The Bridge of Sighs*

X

BOOKS SUGGESTED FOR FURTHER REFERENCE

The following books are suggested for simple, but more comprehensive, reading on those aspects of speech training which have here been passed over without detailed treatment.

GENERAL

Firth, *Speech*, pub. Benn, 6*d*. Series.

HISTORY OF THE LANGUAGE

Wyld, *The Growth of English*, pub. Murray.

VOICE PRODUCTION

Aikin, *The Voice*, pub. Longman.

VERSE SPEAKING

Fogerty, *The Speaking of English Verse*, pub. Dent.

STANDARD ENGLISH

Nicklin, *Standard English Pronunciation*, pub. Oxford, at the Clarendon Press.

Greig, *Breaking Priscian's Head* (To-day and To-morrow Series), pub. Kegan Paul.

PHONETICS

Ward, *The Phonetics of English*, pub. Heffer.
Wyld, *Elementary Exercises in English Grammar* (Chaps. I and II), pub. Oxford, at the Clarendon Press.

SPEECH DEFECTS

Ward, *Defects of Speech*, pub. Dent.

GRAMOPHONE RECORDS

Some mention should be made of the use of gramophone records as models for the student who is anxious to improve his own speech. While there are now available many records made by speakers whose pronunciation might well be studied and imitated, the following selection is given as particularly suitable for this purpose.

The Pronunciation, Rhythm and Intonation of English

*Talks on English Speech by A. Lloyd-James. (5 double-sided records.)
*English Sounds, spoken by A. Lloyd-James. (1 double-sided record.) Published by the Linguaphone Institute.

Extracts from English Prose and Verse

Shakespearian Readings, by John Gielgud. (5 double-sided records.)
Bible Readings. (5 double-sided records.)
*Literary Course in English, recorded by A. Lloyd-James and Kenneth Barnes). (10 double-sided records.)
Published by the Linguaphone Institute.

The Technique of Verse Speaking

The Speaking of Verse, a lecture by John Drinkwater. (2 double-sided records.)
Published by the Columbia Gramophone Co.

* While these records are addressed primarily to foreigners, they may be very profitably used by English students.

XI

APPENDIX: DEFECTIVE SPEECH

As this book is intended for the use of students training to be teachers, it should hardly be necessary to consider defective, as opposed to careless or over-precise speech. The inability to pronounce the English r sound is, however, so commonly found that it will perhaps be legitimate to suggest exercises for the correction of this defect.

The English r (phonetic symbol ɹ) is an alveolar fricative sound, formed in a position very close to ʃ, ʒ, s, z, t, d and n. Speakers who cannot pronounce the sound commonly substitute either (1) a velar or uvular fricative sound (formed by a narrowing between the back of the tongue and the soft palate or uvula), or (2) a sound v^w formed by a narrowing between the upper teeth and lower lip (as for v, but with very little friction), together with a slight simultaneous narrowing between the upper and lower lips (as for w, but without lip rounding).

In (1) and (2) above, the first correction to be made is in tongue position. These defective formations both involve a raising of the back of the tongue, while fricative ɹ requires raising of the tongue tip.

In (2) it will also be necessary to correct the w sound caused by bringing the lips close together. This lip position often persists after the tongue position has been corrected. It is sometimes useful to practise in front of a mirror, with the tip of a pencil held between the front teeth, in order to avoid any bringing together of the lips.

The sound ɹ is best learnt by moving the tongue towards the position required from the position of one of the sounds very near to it. For instance, the student should make the sound of ʃ or ʒ and, while continuing the sound, slightly curl back the tip of the tongue, thus reaching the position of ɹ. The sound can be reached by a similar process from t or d.

In practising the sound, the student should begin with words in which not much movement of the tongue is required from the ɹ position, so that he is able to learn, from the positions of the sounds near by, the exact position and formation of the sound in which he is defective. It will be noted that this principle has dictated the choice of words for practice in the exercises given below.

Exercises for Practice of ɹ (after a consonant and initially)

(1) Easy

shrift	drip	shriek	traitor
shrill	drear	treacle	tray
shrimp	shred	treason	drain
shrink	tread	treat	drake
shrivel	trek	tree	drape
trick	trench	dream	dray
trill	trend	trachea	shrank
trim	tress	tradition	shrapnel
trip	dread	traduce	track
tryst	dredge	trepan	traffic
dribble	dregs	trade	tram
drift	drench	trail	trap
drill	dress	train	trash
drink			

(2) More difficult

shrove	shrug	droop	a wretch
trochee	shrunk	trod	a reach
Trojan	truck	tropic	a ream
trope	trudge	Trossachs	a reaper
droll	trump	trot	a reed
drone	trunk	trough	a reel
shrike	trust	dromedary	a refusal
shrine	drub	drop	a regret
shrive	drudge	dross	a reply
tricycle	drug	trance	a response
tripe	drunk	drama	a return
tripos	trawl	draught	a raid
trite	draw	a rib	a rail
try	Troy	a rill	a rake
drive	shrew	a rink	a rate
dry	shrewd	a ripple	a reign
dryad	troop	a risk	a rag
shroud	troubadour	arrears	a ram
trousers	trousseau	a record	a rank
trout	truant	a remedy	a rap
drown	true	arrest	a rat
drowsy	drool	a wren	a rook
shrub			

(3) Difficult

a rodent	rink	raid	round
a roll	wrist	rail	rouse
a rope	real	rake	rowdy
aright	rear	rate	rub
a rhyme	red	rack	rum
around	rep	rag	run
arouse	rest	ran	rush
a rout	wreck	rat	rut
a rub	wren	wrap	raucous
a run	rare	rook	raw
a rush	reach	rural	roister
a rut	read	road	rude
a roof	ream	roan	rue
a root	reek	rope	roost
a robber	reel	rote	root
a rock	reclaim	row	rule
a rot	redeem	rhyme	robber
a wrong	reduce	rice	rock
rib	regret	right	rod
rick	religion	ripe	rotten
rid	rabies	rise	rasp

Exercises for Practice of ɹ (between vowels)

(1) Easy		(2) More difficult		(3) Difficult[1]	
cheery	Cyril	Kerry	Tory	ferry	barrel
cherry	nearer	caring	snoring	beryl	marry
sherry	jeering	harrow	hoary	merry	sparrow
terrier	hearing	narrow	goring	Pyrrhic	maroon
dearest	lyric	tourist	torrid	miracle	fury
Derry	serrated	jury	sorry	fearing	mooring
sharing	narrate	curate	lorry	beery	furrow
tearing	hay-rick	turret	horrid	fairy	burrow
daring	hairy	hurry	coral	Mary	boring
Syria	clearest	curry		wearing	borrow
				fury	morrow
				spurring	moral

[1] If the defective pronunciation is (2) on p. 88.

INDEX

Printed in the United States
By Bookmasters